INTERNATIONAL CHRISTIAN
GRADUATE UNIVERSITY

AN
EXTENSION SEMINARY
PRIMER

OTHER WILLIAM CAREY LIBRARY BOOKS*

Bradshaw, Malcolm R., CHURCH GROWTH THROUGH EVANGELISM-IN-DEPTH
Cox, Emmett D., THE CHURCH OF THE UNITED BRETHREN IN CHRIST IN SIERRA LEONE
Emery, Kinsler, Walker, Winter, EL SEMINARIO DE EXTENSION: UN MANUAL
Enyart, Paul C., FRIENDS IN CENTRAL AMERICA
Gaxiola, Manuel, LA SERPIENTE Y LA PALOMA
Hedlund, Roger, THE PROTESTANT MOVEMENT IN ITALY: ITS PROGRESS, PROBLEMS, AND PROSPECTS
Holland, Clifton L., THE RELIGIOUS DIMENSION IN SPANISH LOS ANGELES: A PROTESTANT CASE STUDY
McFall, Ernest A., APPROACHING THE NUER OF AFRICA THROUGH THE OLD TESTAMENT
McGavran, Donald A., editor, THE CHURCH GROWTH BULLETIN, VOL. I-V.
Mälüskü, Hilkka, THE CHALLENGE FOR EVANGELICAL MISSIONS TO EUROPE: A SCANDINAVIAN CASE STUDY
Mayers, Marvin K., NOTES ON CHRISTIAN OUTREACH IN A PHILIPPINE COMMUNITY
Mitchell, James Erskine, THE EMERGENCE OF A MEXICAN CHURCH: THE ASSOCIATE REFORMED PRESBYTERIAN CHURCH OF MEXICO
Randall, Max Ward, PROFILE FOR VICTORY: NEW PROPOSALS FOR MISSIONS IN ZAMBIA
Smith, Ebbie C., GOD'S MIRACLES: INDONESIAN CHURCH GROWTH
Subbamma, B. V., NEW PATTERNS FOR DISCIPLING HINDUS: THE NEXT STEP IN ANDHRA PRADESH, INDIA
Swanson, Allen J., TAIWAN: MAINLINE VERSUS INDEPENDENT CHURCH GROWTH, A STUDY IN CONTRASTS
Tippett, A. R., PEOPLES OF SOUTHWEST ETHIOPIA
Wagner, C. Peter, THE PROTESTANT MOVEMENT IN BOLIVIA
Winter, Ralph D., editor, THEOLOGICAL EDUCATION BY EXTENSION
Winter, Ralph D., THE TWENTY-FIVE UNBELIEVABLE YEARS, 1945-1969

*Greater detail and prices are listed in the back of this book.

Ralph R. Covell
C. Peter Wagner

AN
EXTENSION SEMINARY
PRIMER

South Pasadena, California

©Copyright 1971 by Ralph R. Covell and C. Peter Wagner
All rights reserved.

No part of this book may be used or reproduced in any manner whatsoever without written permission, except in the case of brief quotations embodied in critical articles and reviews.

International Standard Book Number: 0-87808-106-2
Library of Congress Catalog Number: 72-168665

Published by the William Carey Library
533 Hermosa Street
South Pasadena, Calif. 91030
Telephone 213-682-2047

PRINTED IN THE UNITED STATES OF AMERICA

INTERNATIONAL CHRISTIAN
GRADUATE UNIVERSITY

To

faithful church leaders in many
lands who are ably teaching and
preaching the Word of God

CONTENTS

Foreword

1   Changing Patterns of Ministerial Training - Wagner   1

2   The Nature of the Church - Covell   15

3   How God Makes Ministers - Wagner   25

4   Jesus, the Model Teacher - Covell   34

5   Why Paul Was Successful in Teaching - Covell   44

6   Forms of Theological Education through History - Covell   52

7   "Training in the Streets" in Chile - Wagner   62

8   The Birth of the Extension Seminary - Wagner   70

9   New Patterns in Bolivia and Colombia - Wagner   77

10   How the Extension Center Works - Wagner   84

11   Old Shortcomings and New Experiments - Wagner   92

12   Educational Principles Underlying Extension Training - Covell   101

13   The Intertext Project and its Progress - Wagner   110

14   The Third Stage in Africa and Asia - Covell   118

15   The Extension Seminary and Church Growth - Covell   127

Bibliography   134

Index   139

FOREWORD

Missions is a process of great variety to promulgate, to expedite and to accomplish Mission. The methods of this process have been different in every country and in every era. The decade of the sixties has been characterized by three emphases in missiology which have assumed a newness of application although they contain much that is out of the past. They are usually entitled as saturation evangelism or evangelism in depth, church growth and theological education by extension.

CAMEO or the Committee to Assist Missionary Education Overseas has been particularly involved in theological education by extension. CAMEO did not originate or create the concept. It received the baton after it had been conceived and was in operation in some three centers in Latin America. CAMEO carried the baton by introducing the concept through workshops among missionary leaders, first in the United States and then by workshops in South America, Africa and Asia. The actual application of the principles of theological education by extension is the responsibility of the educational leaders on the Mission fields of the world, both nationals and missionaries.

The workshops during the summer of 1970 in Taiwan, Vietnam, Indonesia, Singapore and Central India were conducted by C. Peter Wagner and Ralph R. Covell as resource personnel. Following the experiences of this trip they have co-authored this book, An Extension Seminary Primer. The book has grown out of a need. It will serve not only those who shared in the workshops but will be a continuing guide for any educational workers and administrators who are involved in or who are considering the viability of this new technique.

The two authors are peculiarly fitted to write on this subject, complementing each other in their contribution.

Peter Wagner from Cochabamba, Bolivia, is the Associate Director of the Andes Evangelical Mission. He is one of the pioneers of the strategy of theological education by extension. He writes therefore both from the experiential and the administrative standpoint. Mr. Wagner has served in a teaching capacity at the School of Missions at Fuller Theological Seminary. Dr. Ralph Covell, now the head of the department of Missions at the Denver Conservative Baptist Theological Seminary, was a missionary for one term in China and for three terms in Taiwan. His work in Taiwan, in addition to the translation of the New Testament, included the founding and development of a Bible institute into a seminary for training Christian leaders in that country. His background in Asiatic education is a fitting supplement to Wagner's Latin American finesse.

This book, although not massive, is thorough. Some will question the inclusion of Biblical Studies in Chapters 2, 3, 4 and 5. The authors' experience in five Asian workshops indicated that this material is the foundation on which to build the theoretical and practical treatment of the subject.

The writers have been willing to face the criticisms that are continually expressed. A reading of the book will help the lethargic and ignorant to change with the expressed information and knowledge. There are other basic criticisms that will be met with the use and modifications of the techniques. The understanding of the procedures will come as the methods are applied in specific areas.

The term "seminary" is used with its Latin American connotation, which covers a much wider area than in other parts of the world and includes many levels of educational training. Perhaps the term "theological education" is more comprehensive and will fit the situation for training leaders as found in Africa and Asia.

The term "primer" is well selected for the title. The book covers the historical beginnings of the movement giving the early pioneers' experiences as they made their first mistakes but came through to a sophisticated approach. The introduction of the concept through the workshops in America and on the continents of South America, Africa and Asia was the avenue by which the methods and values of the strategy were spread among the missionaries and nationals throughout the world for their consideration.

In addition to the historical facts that are valuable in such a primer, the basics for carrying out education are well outlined, usually in connection with actual situations.

Foreword　　　　　　　　　　　　　　　　　　　　　　　　　　*xi*

　　Those who have read Dr. Ralph Winter's <u>Theological Education by Extension</u> will want to read this book. Its treatment of the subject is supplementary to Winter's coverage. Those who read this Primer will wish to complete their understanding of extension seminary education by reading what Winter has prepared. These books complement each other. It is not an either/or situation; it is a both/and.

　　The timing of this work is appropriate. During the next decade we are convinced this form of education, possibly modified in many ways, will be used in all parts of the world. The book therefore will be in demand, and we are grateful to these men for taking the time from their busy schedules to write when the influence and knowledge gained during their world trip is fresh at hand.

RAYMOND B. BUKER, SR.
Coordinator, CAMEO

1
CHANGING PATTERNS OF MINISTERIAL TRAINING

A modest experiment with a new form of ministerial training in Guatemala in 1962 has, within a decade, not only drawn the attention of theological educators world-wide, but also caused many to rethink their patterns and presuppositions for theological education. As Ralph Winter, one of the architects of the extension seminary, says, "We do at least now have a movement on our hands."[1]

The movement, quite naturally, spread first of all from Guatemala to other Latin American countries, notably Colombia, Bolivia and Brazil. Soon CAMEO (the joint committee of Interdenominational Foreign Mission Association and Evangelical Foreign Missions Association to Assist Missionary Education Overseas), under the leadership of Raymond Buker, Sr., became interested in the concept and sponsored a workshop in Wheaton in 1968, well attended by missionaries from most parts of the world. This in turn produced invitations for similar workshops in Asia and Africa, the first round of them being held in the Summer of 1970. England and Spain have workshops scheduled for early 1971.

From its present application in younger churches, interest in extension theological education is now increasing in U.S.A. seminaries. An excellent study by F. Ross Kinsler of the Presbyterian Seminary in Guatemala has outlined ways in which extension principles could help overcome certain deficiencies in U.S. theological education.[2] Taking a broader view which includes developments in secular education, Ted Ward of Michigan State University has observed that "theological education by extension is rapidly moving to a leadership position among the educational movements of the day."[3]

In the secular world, where educators have realized that their institutions will not be able to sustain growth rates equal to those of the population explosion, methods which have been found helpful in the extension seminary are being applied. In January of 1971 "The Open University" in England will begin courses leading to a B.A. degree. As *The Expository Times* reports, "This will prove a real godsend to older men and women who feel equipped to proceed to degree work, but cannot absent themselves from the duties which provide their livelihood, or to women who cannot discard the responsibilities of home and family."[4]

The Israeli government for a number of years has attempted to teach Hebrew to new immigrants by "taking the school to adults." The pilot projects consisted of residential schools, but when it became obvious that these would not keep pace with the needs, an extension program was inaugurated. By 1965 half of the immigrant students (10,500 of 21,350) were studying in extension centers called *"ulpaniyot."*[5]

CHANGING PATTERNS OF THE CHURCH

One of the phenomena of today's rapidly-changing world has been a noticeable change in patterns of the church. The New Testament does not purport to give us a master blueprint for church form. Although some still do consider a particular church structure "more biblical" than others, a new openness toward differing forms of the church seems to be characteristic of Christians today.

The church, in its simplest form, is where the believers are. When the IVCF group meets on campus, for example, this is a type of functional church meeting. Christian businessmen, nurses, military officers, scientists, and others who have common secular interests form associations which (in spite of predictable denials) become kinds of churches outside the church. Some interdenominational missions in foreign cities become functional churches when they hold their own Sunday worship in English. Organizations such as the Gideons or Young Life or Christian Endeavor have functioned as churches for some people.

Home Bible studies are becoming popular in some areas, and are considered their "church" by many who attend them. Groups of Christians in the charismatic movement sometimes meet outside their own church buildings and programs. If a conflict occurs, some will feel so loyal to their ad hoc meetings that they prefer to split from their traditional church rather than give up the new form they have discovered. The term "underground church" is now commonplace.

In Red China faithful Christians can meet secretly in groups which must not exceed two or three--a form of the church reminiscent of the catacombs. In Indonesia groups of evangelical Christians from the Reformed Protestant Churches have begun what they call "by-pass" groups. They think they are bypassing the church, but in reality they have developed a new form of church. The Philippine Congress on Evangelism recommended the formation of 10,000 "cell groups" as the basis of future church growth there. These cell groups will not look much like our traditional churches.

Rapidly-growing cities with limited real estate such as Hong Kong and Singapore have brought about the development of still another form--"churches in the flats." Mac Bradshaw anticipates that "land area for church buildings will be scarce and prohibitively priced. Life patterns for high-rise flat dwellers will not likely be conducive to crossing town for the 11 a.m. Sunday service."[6] The newly-emerging forms of house churches which own no real estate of their own may even be closer to New Testament patterns than the "cathedral on the corner," according to Bradshaw.

Many missiologists believe that we are now on the threshold of the greatest ingathering into the Christian Church that the world has yet experienced. McGavran, with his characteristic optimism, has recently said that we are today witnessing "the sunrise of missions." President Doan-van-Mieng of the Vietnamese National Church is entirely serious when he claims that the Lord has spoken to him and to the church he leads to set their long-range goal at winning ten million Vietnamese for Christ. If these men prove to be right, this degree of accelerated church growth will undoubtedly produce new sets of changing patterns of the church. Leaders will do well to be alert for them.

CHANGING PATTERNS OF THE MINISTRY

As Christians recognize and encourage changing patterns of the church, they realize that an immediate corollary of this will be new forms of the ministry. Bradshaw says that in the exploding cities of Asia, "full-time ministers will no doubt continue to be needed. Yet the brunt of the responsibility for shepherding the small house congregations will of necessity fall upon the shoulders of a new task force of semi-professional ministers . . . Self-supporting status will be essential because most flat churches will be too small in numbers to support a full-time pastor."[7]

From the other side of the world, Mario Rivas, President of the Bolivian Baptist Union, makes a plea for a new dynamic nationalism in his church. It may be necessary "to give up the idea of a paid ministry," he suggests. "Let's forget the idealistic position of a full-time pastorate if the situation so demands. Let's get out into the community and work like other men, earning our daily bread through radio broadcasting, teaching, public offices, and above that offer our talents for the glory of God. Many pastors are doing it already."[8]

In a recent book on Indonesia, Ebbie Smith urges his Baptist colleagues there to set as a goal the planting of 50 new churches a year. But he recognizes that "Baptists cannot provide places of worship and trained pastors for fifty new congregations a year for the next ten years."[9] Thus, he recommends house churches and unpaid pastors. "Unpaid or slightly paid non-seminary trained pastors should be recognized and allowed to function fully as pastors, leading their congregations with full freedom, drawing their authority from the Lord and the congregation they lead."[10] This type of creative thinking is by no means confined to Bradshaw, Rivas, and Smith. On all six continents Christian leaders have become convinced that a total rethinking of the form and function of the ministry is long overdue.

Basic to the newer ideas of the ministry is the concept of ordination. Some younger churches have found themselves with a two-level hierarchy they had neither planned nor desired—ordained and unordained ministers. Functionally they are doing the same job in many cases, but for one reason or other ordination is denied to some, relegating them to a second-class status. Some churches insist that ordained ministers be full-time, thus excluding the biblical pattern of a tent-making ministry. Educational levels form another rather artificial barrier in certain circumstances. Institutions have been created with academic levels which exclude many functional pastors on principle. In some cases, more emphasis seems to be placed on academic attainment than on spiritual gifts.

The widespread concern in many younger churches to "raise the standards of the ministry" seems to be somewhat misguided, since again it is usually linked directly to certain academic levels. An uncritical application of this principle could well serve to cripple the ministry rather than upgrade it. The use of the term "lay pastors" is well-intentioned, but tends to accentuate their second-class rating. In one church I know this was carried to such an extreme that, whereas both ordained and unordained pastors could pronounce the benediction, only the ordained pastors were allowed to raise their hands while doing it!

Raising the standards of the ministry usually has a corollary: the desire to "upgrade the seminary." This, unwisely, has become one of the major goals of theological educators in many parts of the world. It is commonly interpreted as meaning raising the admission requirements another notch, and if possible eliminating a lower notch. The net result is that the gap between first and second class pastors is widened even more, and the institution runs the risk of educating pastors right out of the system. This is one reason why so many of the best educated ministers in the younger churches buy one-way tickets to the U.S.A. They no longer fit in their own system.

More important than higher and higher academic requirements should be spiritual and cultural standards. A man of God who is fully accepted by his peers as a leader, who has spiritual gifts which equip him for his task, and who leads his church forward in winning people to Christ and planting new churches, is the man who should be studying in our institutions regardless of his previous academic opportunities. Unhappily, many who fit this description have not been eligible for our seminaries, and therefore have been excluded from the possibility of ordination.

The vested interests of the ordained clergy have at times prevented broader concepts of the ministry. In some cases, consciously or unconsciously, ordained men have created something of a "preachers' union" and decreed a closed shop. Since both the mission subsidy fund and the number of well-paying churches are limited, new competition is discouraged in one way or another. The danger of this mentality is evident, especially when applied to planting new churches. Some denominations discourage the organization of a church until a pastor is available, thus making the rate of church multiplication dependent upon the ability of a seminary to produce graduates. This thinking needs to be changed. It can become an unwholesome deterrent to healthy church growth.

CHANGING PATTERNS OF LEADERSHIP TRAINING

Once changing patterns of the church and the ministry are recognized, the problem of ministerial training must be faced. Here again we find changing patterns in today's world. Both Bradshaw and Smith recommend for their specific areas of Asia what is now known as the extension seminary. This has been used by some institutions in Latin America since 1962, and estimates indicate that some fifty institutions there are using these methods to train something over 2,000 students. As to Africa, Gerald Bates of Burundi writes, "The extension seminary and its use of programmed learning offer a viable alternative to some present forms of education which are falling far short in the matter of leadership training, particularly for the pastorate, in Africa."[11]

Recent studies have shown that, in spite of vast cultural differences between them, churches in Asia, Africa and Latin America share with remarkable correlation a set of deficiencies in their traditional theological education programs. To one degree or another these might be corrected by adapting extension seminary principles to their particular situation.

What are these principles?

PHILOSOPHY OF EXTENSION

The extension seminary involves first of all a change in mental attitude for those who have been involved in traditional institutions. If we were to seek a slogan for this change, I would call it "the humanization of theological education."

This intentionally implies that our past efforts at training the ministry have not quite been human enough. I think that most of us who honestly examine ourselves on this matter will admit that this has often been true. At least the recent workshops in Asia have reflected a new openness on the part of both missionaries and nationals to recognize past shortcomings and face the future more realistically. This process is part of what Ted Ward calls "a profound alteration of institutions of long standing and rich tradition."[12]

For one thing we have tended to be institution-centered rather than person-centered. We have wrongly asked "how?" before asking "whom?" We have started with an institutional structure which we may have adapted to a degree to the culture of our particular field, but which was, nevertheless heavily laden with inevitable cultural baggage. Then we have set up certain requirements for admission and opened the doors. Those who could fit our requirements could come in, but the others stayed out. In other words, the person to be trained had to conform to our institution.

The extension philosophy involves starting with the person rather than the institution. If a given person should be receiving ministerial training, the institution should see that he gets it, according to this new mentality. No possible alteration of the structure of the institution should be discounted which will enable more of God's chosen men to take theological studies. As the seminary or Bible school conforms to the student to be trained rather than vice-versa, it is to that degree "humanizing theological education."

Theological educators are now coming to recognize that the task of the seminary is not to <u>make</u> leaders. As John Meadowcroft of West Pakistan puts it, "By some kind of metamorphosis, a young fellow who has no qualities of leadership is expected to emerge from the chrysalis of the seminary as a 'leader of the community.' And he also considers himself to be. The fact, however, is that nothing will make a man a leader if he does not possess the attributes already."[13] The calling of the seminary is to <u>train</u> the leaders that God has already made. If this is admitted, the question prior to all others becomes: Whom do we teach?

That God, and not man, sovereignly distributes gifts of the ministry to the members of the body of Christ "as it hath pleased Him" is clear from I Corinthians 12. The task of the church is not to endow these gifts, but rather to recognize them, help develop them, admonish Christians to use them, and publically authorize their use through the laying on of hands. Our seminaries and Bible schools should set their sights on this objective--training men and women who are the gifted ones of God for the ministry: pastors, teachers, evangelists, and others.

Especially in the younger, rapidly-growing churches of the world, these gifts are most evident in men and women somewhat older than the students we have usually been training. Cultures which respect age more than we do in contemporary U.S.A. ordinarily will not allow a younger person to assume a position of true leadership (although at times a leadership title may be granted). Qualifications for leadership usually include maturity, marriage, a family, the ability to earn a living through a contribution to the community, and church responsibilities properly executed. Some of these leaders have been recognized by their people but cannot be ordained by their churches because they are unable to conform to any known institution. Others have had some theological training earlier in life and have been ordained; but with the rising standards of education, they feel the need of more studies. A leader of the Indian church says: "The average pastor in India does not know how to lead a soul to Christ or to preach expository messages." Those of us in theological education need to be concerned about this kind of situation.

This points up the need for in-service training, perhaps to an even greater degree than for pre-service training. Nevertheless our concentration to the present has largely been on the pre-service variety of training. The recognition of this basic principle was one of the factors that sparked the Presbyterian Seminary in Guatemala to launch the first extension program eight years ago. In one of the pioneer documents of the extension seminary movement, James Emery of Guatemala said, "The people who most need the training are not those who traditionally attend the seminary, but those of the larger group who are more mature, and with experience."[14]

HOW THE SEMINARY EXTENDS

As the extension seminary principles have developed over the past few years, the sense in which seminaries have "extended" has become clearer.

From the beginning it should be kept in mind that we are suggesting an *extension*, not an *extermination* of the present structures. Years of sharing extension principles with others have taught us that most of the initial opposition to the new ideas comes from those who interpret the extension program as a threat to their existing institutions. They have made an "either-or" case of extension versus residence. This is unfair and hasty. The two programs are complementary, not contradictory. Most (although not all) residential institutions are serving a very useful function and should be continued. But few (or perhaps none) are doing as much as they *should* or *could* do. In order better to accomplish their goal of training the ministry for the church, they should think in terms of extending their present ministry.

Theological educators who are willing to become student-centered rather than institution-centered in their outlook will want to consider extending their present structures in six ways:

1. <u>Geographical extension</u>. This refers to the place or places where students are taught. Due to any number of circumstances, many gifted church leaders cannot leave their own homes and move into a residential institution. If they are to be trained, then, the institution must somehow move to them. This may mean that a professor in Bolivia travels six hours on the train to meet a group of students every week, or that his counterpart in West Kalimantan contracts the Missionary Aviation Fellowship plane for two days a week to visit three centers, or that the students from one area meet their teacher

under a bridge as they did in Guatemala. By whatever means are necessary, the professor moves out to his students.

Some professors, accustomed to the more sedentary and contemplative life of the ivory tower will say, "this is not for me!" But scores of others are saying, "this is what I have been looking for."

    2. <u>Extension in time</u>. Schedules in the extension seminary are drawn up *after* asking the student: When can you study? I know of one weekly meeting at 6:00 a.m., another at 10:00 p.m., and others in between. Urban centers usually meet at night since students are tied to strict daily schedules. Rural centers often meet during the day since farmers' schedules are more flexible. After the sun sets, farmers usually think more of bed than of books.

The time factor is not only important as to the hour, but also as to the seasons. One center operating among potato farmers inadvisedly scheduled its courses to run through the potato harvest. It soon had to close down and rearrange the program. Whereas ordinarily all extension centers adhere to the academic year of the base institution, ample room for adjustment must be allowed.

Some students have more leisure time for study than others. Thus the speed at which students complete their studies will have to vary. This variation is usually not made according to the rate at which a student completes a given subject, but rather according to the number of subjects the student handles in any given semester. If he can afford six hours a week, he can take just one subject, but if he can afford eighteen hours a week, he may take three.

    3. <u>Cultural extension</u>. As the insights of cultural anthropology filter down to grass roots, missionary educators have become more aware of patterns of culture and sub-culture all over the world. Even people living within the same city, group themselves into distinct sub-cultures, as a short drive from Beverly Hills, through Watts and to East Los Angeles would prove. Molds of thinking in each sub-culture are different, and proper theological education will be tailor-made for each one. Institutions that are not extended will often require that a student from one culture take his training within another one. Experience has shown that this cultural extraction is not ideal.

In the July, 1970, Asia Evangelical Theological Consultation held in Singapore, Dr. Ogill Kim of Korea said, "The training of national theological faculty members can best be done in their own countries. We must get rid of the mentality of being students of Western theology. Asians are leaders of the theology of Asia."[15] Professor Bong Rin Ro of the Discipleship Training Center in Singapore laments the fact that "many Asian Christians uphold the West as their theological model. Thousands of young people have made an exodus, particularly to the U.S. for their education."[16]

Observations like these do not relate only to those vast cultural differences between the Eastern and Western Hemispheres. They exist also within the same country. Leaders of rural churches in South Viet Nam, for example, were recently discussing the problems that sending their ministerial candidates to study in the city raised. They said, "When our men return to the country they are not the same. They want their salary in cash, not in rice and chickens; they won't walk through the rice paddies because they will get their trousers wet; they are not even able to sit and talk with us because they have brought their city schedules back with them and no longer have any time."

The extension seminary attempts to adapt to people who need training by making sure that the teaching is relevant to the culture in which they have been called to minister in the future. This is one reason why the leaders of the Latin American Intertext program have rather firmly insisted that their materials all be prepared originally in either Spanish or Portuguese in spite of a great deal of pressure from other parts of the world to do them in English. Not only will this provide material in the most useful languages there, but it will also tend to force authors to develop their materials in thought patterns characteristic of the culture of their students.

The extension seminary enables students to take full theological training while continuing to live within their own culture. This reduces the danger of deculturization, known in one of its international aspects as the "brain drain." While it is true that many examples of dedicated people who have studied in a second culture and have returned successfully to the first can be found, most theological educators and church leaders will agree that the trend is in the opposite direction.

4. _Academic extension_. It has already been mentioned that many of us have fallen into the mentality that certain minimum academic requirements are necessary for the Christian ministry, and that these requirements should be universally applied. Further analysis, however, will probably indicate that academic standards for the ministry are better determined

by the academic levels of the people in the pews than by the seminary board. It may be true that college and seminary are basic for a U.S.A. suburban pastor, and that seminaries now need to replace the B.D. with a professional doctorate to keep their graduates on an academic par with the increasing number of Ph.D.'s in their congregations. This standard is not necessary among the mountain peoples of Taiwan, however, nor perhaps even for effective ministry in the black ghettos of the inner cities of the U.S.A.

Thousands of leaders of third world churches have been able to attain only minimal levels of general education, and they find themselves in no position to return to school. Should these men be excluded from theological training on those grounds, when God himself has placed them in the ministry? The seminary must extend itself to such men. Some extension programs have geared theological education to as low as second grade levels, especially when the church in question will grant ordination (or whatever form of ministerial recognition is employed) to these leaders. Others, such as the Presbyterians in Guatemala, have developed subsidiary programs to raise the general educational level to sixth grade before they begin theological training. Either way extends the seminary academically.

5. Economic extension. The expense involved in training men for ordination (whether this term is understood formally or functionally is irrelevant here) in the younger churches is higher than many of us may think. A competent observer has recently stated that on a world scale the cost of this educational system may be second only to that of training physicians in the U.S.A. When the cost of providing missionary professors, buildings and grounds, the low student-teacher ratios, and the high drop-out quotient are considered, this might well be the case.

On most mission fields where indigenous church principles are applied, missions have found that one of the last aspects of the church-related work which can be turned over to the churches is the ministerial training program. This is due largely to the economic structure which is often entirely out of keeping with what the churches can afford. If a less expensive way to train ministers could be found, some of the national churches could exercise greater responsibility in this crucially important aspect of their development toward full maturity.

The extension seminary may prove to be a step in that direction. Studies that have been made indicate a reduction in costs, although more research is still needed. The George Allan Theological Seminary in Bolivia, for example, has found that their urban residence program costs about $90.00 annually per student-subject, the rural residence program about $30.00 per student-subject, and the extension program about $15.00 per student-subject. Other than the modest initial cost of setting up the extension centers, most of this sum represents travel for professors. The students pay their own way--travel expenses, room and board, and textbooks. They also help reduce general costs by paying a monthly tuition. This sounds like something that any church can afford.

6. <u>Ecclesiastical extension</u>. The widespread divorce of the seminary from the local church has been recognized by leaders of many denominations in recent years. As Sam Rowen says, "The development or training of Christians should take place in a genuine church-life situation. Only as the church becomes aware of the need for the systematic study of the Word of God will there be developed the proper attitude towards theological training . . . . Theological training should be church-centered."[17]

Until recently, few had been able to suggest ways and means to reverse the trend of separation. But placing theological training back in the local church has been a welcome by-product of some extension seminaries. In many cases classes are actually held on church premises. Seminary professors visit the churches and interact with church members as well as with students, keeping themselves in direct touch with their thinking and attitudes. This makes them ever so much more effective as teachers. Students, for their part, are not extracted from their local church for an extended period of time, but they continually relate their studies to the realistic conditions of the grass-roots level.

NOTES FOR CHAPTER 1

1. Ralph D. Winter, ed., Theological Education by Extension, South Pasadena, William Carey Library, 1969, p. xvii.

2. F. Ross Kinsler, "Extend the Seminaries," chapter in Theological Education by Extension, Ralph D. Winter, ed., pp. 245-255.

3. Ted and Margaret Ward, Programmed Instruction for Theological Education by Extension, CAMEO, East Lansing, 1970, p. 115.

4. "The Open University," The Expository Times, April, 1970, p. 224.

5. Ministry of Education and Culture, Israel, School Comes To Adults, Jerusalem, 1965, p. 57.

6. Malcolm Bradshaw, Theological Education by Extension, leaflet.

7. Ibid.

8. Mario Rivas, "Nueva Vision de la Iglesia Nacional," article in Chasqui, Los Angeles, September, 1970.

9. Ebbie Smith, God's Miracles: Indonesian Church Growth, South Pasadena, William Carey Library, 1970, p. 195.

10. Ibid., pp. 195-196.

11. Gerald Bates, The Extension Seminary, Its Potential for African Young Churches, mimeographed paper, Lansing, Michigan State University, 1970, 13 pp.

12. Ward, Programmed Instruction for Theological Education by Extension, p. 115.

13. John G. Meadowcroft, Theological Education by Extension, mimeographed paper, Gujranwala, West Pakistan, 1970, p. 6.

14. James H. Emery, "The Preparation of Leaders in a Ladino-Indian Church," Practical Anthropology, Vol. 10, No. 3, 1963, pp. 127-134.

15. Okgill Kim, quoted in privately-circulated minutes of the Asia Evangelical Theological Consultation, Singapore, July 5-7, 1970.

16. Bong Rin Ro, "Some Thoughts on the Future of Theological Education in Asia," *The Asian Challenge*, Vol. 2, September, 1970, p. 49.

17. Samuel F. Rowen, "Let's Train the Right People," *Whitened Harvest*, Fall, 1968, supplement.

2

THE NATURE OF THE CHURCH

Theological education cannot be discussed without considering the church and its ministry. The nature of the church determines the nature of the ministry. The nature of the ministry dictates the nature and form of theological education. As we understand the nature of the church we know who we train, why we train them, how we train them, and what is the content of our training. Each facet of the nature of the church should tell us something about theological education.

In the Acts of the Apostles those who comprise the church are called by many different names. For example, we note (6:1) that the followers of Jesus are referred to as disciples. They have a relationship to Christ of learning. They have come to him and are learning from him (Matthew 11:28). Those who follow Christ are also called brethren. They belong to the family of God through their relationship with Jesus Christ. This family of disciples were first called Christians at Antioch (11:26). This was not a self-chosen name. The followers of Christ made it so evident they were related to him that they were called *Christ*ians. The disciples are also referred to as those belonging to the way (9:2), an undoubted reference to Jesus' statement, "I am the way, the truth and the life," (John 14:6). Finally, those who followed Jesus are called "those who believed" (4:32). The early church, in its initial experience as recorded for us in the book of Acts, is made up of those who have made a definite personal commitment to Christ.

Despite these many terms being used to refer to the followers of Jesus, the word "church" is not used extensively in Acts. Its primary meaning is to refer to believers in one particular locality who have come together to worship God, to fellowship with one another and to serve Christ. The concept of an institutional church is often rejected today. In this view, the church is thought of as merely a spiritual organism. Idealistically, and even theologically, this may be very true, but when we look at the church in the New Testament, we see that it has a body and is very visible, and tangible. Its locality, its nationality, its particularity are essential marks of its very being. It is not comparable to a school of Stoic or Epicurean philosophers whose existence in a given place is quite accidental.

But we do note in Acts that there are a few places where the church is referred to in terms which go beyond a merely local sense. For example, Luke records (9:31) that "the church throughout all Judea and Galilee and Samaria had peace and was built up; and walking in the fear of the Lord and in the comfort of the Holy Spirit it was multiplied." The term is used in such a way as to embrace all of the people of God in these several localities. Paul reminds the elders of the Ephesian church (20:28) to, "Take heed to yourselves and to all the flock in which the Holy Spirit has made you guardians, to feed the church of the Lord which he purchased with his own blood." Since the church is described as belonging to the Lord and as having been purchased with his own blood, it refers to a group beyond one local congregation.

The church, then, in Acts is that group of people who are *disciples* of Christ, who are *brethren* in him, who have the name *Christian*, who have identified themselves with the Way, Jesus Christ, and who have committed themselves as believers to him. Every type of person and every level of society is included within this community. There are Greek-speaking Hebrews, Hebrew-speaking Hebrews, and Greek-speaking Gentiles, who, because of their past association with Jewish synagogues, are God-fearers. Also within this fellowship are Greek-speaking Gentiles, who have come directly to faith in Christ from a life of superstitious idolatry.

What do we learn about theological education when we note the heterogeneity of the church and its inclusion within itself of various sub-cultures and of many different levels of society? One apparent observation is that leaders must be trained within each group represented in the church fellowship. This will dictate a multi-cultural approach difficult to accomplish in our present type of seminary program.

The church has a three-fold relationship, It is a community related vertically to the triune God. Internal relationships knit the church into a tight family fellowship. Finally, the church is related outwardly to the world where it is to serve and proclaim the message of Christ.

Of first importance is the relationship of the church to the triune God. The church is a fellowship comprised of those who have been called by God the Father to his salvation. Peter enunciates clearly that "you are a chosen race, a royal priesthood, a holy nation, God's own people, that you may declare the wonderful deeds of him who called you out of darkness into his marvelous light," (I Peter 2:9). The church is a called people. They have been taken from the bondage of sin, from the sphere of ignorance toward God, from a state of darkness, and they have been brought by God into his marvelous light.

They are aware of the fact that the condition in which they now exist is different from the one they formerly had. Much discussion is occurring today about the possibility of a person being an anonymous Christian. He is living his life for Christ and he is related to Christ, we are told, even though he may not have heard anything about Christ. This experience was not familiar to members of the New Testament church. They had a self-consciousness that they were God's own people, commissioned to declare his wonderful deeds in the world.

The church is a community which belongs to Jesus Christ. We note again in Acts 20:28, "Take heed to yourselves and to all the flock, in which the Holy Spirit has made you guardians, to feed the church of the Lord which he purchased with his own blood." The church is a redeemed people, neither belonging to nor existing for itself. Paul unites these two aspects of the church's calling by God and its possession by Jesus Christ in I Thessalonians 2:14, where he refers to "The churches of God in Christ Jesus which are in Judea."

In the third place, the church is a community related to the Holy Spirit. It is a charismatic community. This truth is very evident from the second chapter of Acts. Those gathered together in Jerusalem have created a great stir. Each one has spoken in his own language, the wonderful words of God. Bystanders are amazed, and do not know what this means. Peter, using the Old Testament prophecies recorded in Joel, reminds them that this is the fulfillment of God's promises. The early church was conscious of the fact that the Holy Spirit had come upon them that he had given to them a specific work to do and that he had equipped them with particular gifts to do this work. Theirs was the original mission impossible. And yet, being equipped supernaturally by the power of the Holy Spirit, it became mission accomplished.

Charles Dodd points out that a part of the givenness of the gospel, a very central part of the *kerygma* preached by the early church, was the fact that this was the age of fulfillment, the age of the Holy Spirit.[1] Because of his presence they were not merely a human institution trying vainly to be "do-gooders." Rather they were God's chosen community, redeemed by Jesus Christ and filled with the Holy Spirit for a world-shaking task.

The church trains men and women who have this relationship to Christ how to proclaim and to live effectively the message of reconciliation. However, the task of training will be selective. It will concentrate its efforts on those whose Spirit-given gifts clearly evidence their Divine calling.

In the second place, those who belong to this charismatic community, purchased by Jesus Christ and called by God the Father, have a very intimate relationship with each other. The church is not merely a sum of separate individuals who have made a decision for Christ. It is a corporate body, and when we are in Christ we are more than single individuals--we are members of a family with brothers and sisters in him. Our entire life must be lived in relationship to other members of this fellowship. This is of the very nature of the church and not peripheral to its being. Since the church is a corporate fellowship, the exhortations of the New Testament are exhortations to a social life within this community. We are to have fellowship one with another (I John 1). We are exhorted to love one another, to submit one to another, to help one another, to exhort one another, and to confess our sins one to another.

These commands are not easy to obey. It is far easier to live our Christian lives to ourselves without any intimate relationship to our brothers or to our sisters in Christ. And yet it is through this very process that Christians are socialized and brought to maturity within the family of Jesus Christ.

The family functions as a socializing agent within our society. In my own family we have three boys, all teen-agers. Each has his own room. We get along wonderfully well while separate and with a minimum of contact with each other. When we are together too much, tension, dissensions and difficulties arise. However, through these problems and the consequent maturity deriving from such relationships our boys are socialized, they learn the values of their culture, and they are prepared to live effective lives in society.

The ethics to which we are exhorted in the New Testament are not privatized but social. Note, for example, how Paul exhorts Christians at Ephesus that "with all lowliness and meekness, with patience forbearing one another in love," they should be "eager to maintain the unity of the spirit in the bond of peace," (Ephesians 4:2-3). You cannot be lowly, meek and patient all by yourself. You cannot forbear one another in love by yourself. You cannot maintain the unity of the spirit merely as an isolated Christian. All of these exhortations take the family life, the social life of the Christian in his relationship with other Christians, as a foundational truth.

We constantly sense a need for each other. In Romans 1, Paul explains to the church at Rome that he wishes to bring a spiritual gift to them, and then he adds, "That is, that we may be mutually encouraged by each others faith, both yours and mine" (Romans 1:12). He was an experienced messenger of the gospel who had established many churches for Jesus Christ. He was mature in the Christian faith. Those to whom he was writing were young Christians who had not engaged in any extensive activities in the proclamation of the gospel. Despite this, Paul felt that not only would he be able to strengthen their faith, but that their faith, as well, could encourage and strengthen him. This indicates his concept of the nature of the church as a mutual fellowship of those belonging to Jesus Christ within this community of faith. None could grow to maturity without the help of the other. If any were weak, this was the fault of all. If any were strong, this also was the result of a common effort. The church is a family, and we cannot understand what its nature is or what task God has given to it if we lose sight of its corporate nature.

What are the implications for theological education of the corporate nature of the church? For one thing, it is from within this close-knit church fellowship that leaders will emerge. Even as is the case within a family in society, a certain time is needed for the members to develop to maturity. Young men who have had limited contact with the church as a fellowship, and who are then separated from it by a long period of preparation, will not easily be able to give mature leadership. Paul exhorts us to "lay hands quickly on no one" (I Timothy 3:6). In our enthusiasm to train young leaders who have not had sufficient time for mature development within the fellowship of the church, we are coming very close to violating this command.

In the second place, we do need pastors within the church who have the ability to nurture, to admonish, to rebuke, to exhort, and to lead the flock of God.

The church's third relationship is outward toward the world. The church of Jesus Christ, by its very nature, is in the world. Thus, Paul writes to the church at Corinth, at Philippi, at Colossae, and at Thessalonica. Not only is the church *in* the world, it is also separated *from* the world. More specifically, it is separated from the evil of the world. For this reason, the New Testament emphasizes the church as a holy community, a group of people separated to the purposes of God and collectively referred to as saints. An obvious tension exists between the concept of being *in* the world and of being separated *from* the world. Jesus Christ felt this tension in his great intercessory prayer when he prayed, "I have given them my word and the world has hated them because they are not of the world even as I am not of the world. I do not pray that thou shouldst take them out of the world but that thou shouldst keep them from the evil one. They are not of the world even as I am not of the world" (John 17:14-16).

The balance between the church's presence *in* the world and its separation *from* the world comes from its commission to go *into* the world. Again Jesus prays to the Father, "As thou didst send me into the world so I have sent them into the world," (John 17:18). The church has a relationship to the triune God. It has a responsibility to all the family members within its own fellowship. The church has a mission to the world that is best epitomized by the words of Jesus Christ, when he said, "Go therefore and make disciples of all nations, baptizing them in the name of the Father and of the Son and of the Holy Spirit, teaching them to observe all that I have commanded you; and lo, I am with you always, to the close of the age," (Matthew 28:19-20). Jesus Christ sent his disciples out to proclaim the gospel, to make disciples of men and women, and then to teach them and to train them to live in the world and to serve him within this world.

Unfortunately, it has been easy for the church to develop a ghetto complex. In trying to be separated from the world, Christians have isolated themselves from the world and have insulated themselves from all of those contacts which are natural bridges for the communication of the gospel. Their life has been centered upon themselves. They have been preoccupied with developing a relationship to God and mutual relationships within the fellowship of faith, but they have forgotten the mission to the world. Nearly everything that some members of the church do is within the context of faith. Several hours a week are spent at the church sanctuary. Their children may be sent to Christian schools. The father may belong to the Christian business men's club. He may play on a Christian softball team or a Christian bowling team. All of the relationships of the parents and of the children are with Christian people. No time or energy is left for them to consider how they might have an effective contact with people of the world, in order to live within the world the message of Jesus Christ.

At this point the nature of the church is similar to the nature of Jesus Christ himself. He is the God-man. He has two natures, the human and the divine, which can neither be separated nor combined. Only by coming into the world in such a fashion was he able to effect the work of redemption. In like fashion, the church has a relationship to God and to the world. These cannot be separated and neither can they be combined. Only as this balance and tension is maintained is the church able effectively to perform its ministry.

What does it mean to theological education that the church is in the world? First of all, it means that leaders must be trained who are world-oriented in their thinking rather than merely fellowship-oriented. One person has remarked that the early church was able to turn the world upside-down because they themselves had first been turned inside-out. A frequent statement heard when theological education is being discussed is, "all of our churches have pastors. Therefore, we do not need to have a program of training more leaders." This statement reflects the church that is turned in upon itself. The basic question is, "What can we do in order that we might have more churches?" This demands a program of evangelism.

Take, for example, the Presbyterian church in Taiwan. In 1954 it launched a program which was called "Double the Church Movement." At that time the Presbyterians had 400 churches on the plains of Taiwan. Through an extensive program of evangelism, they had increased these 400 churches to 800 by 1964. This type of emphasis upon our mission in the world will demand a particular type of leadership--a leadership that has its focus toward the world and not merely inward upon its own edification and nurture. The type of leaders adequate for this type of ministry will be mature men who themselves are thoroughly immersed in the world, who understand it, who have contacts with its people, and who are living out their lives within real situations.

A second implication follows. If we have a task within the world, it is more natural to train people where they are in order that they not lose the contacts they have. James Hopewell, formerly of the Theological Education Fund, has observed that if we were to start all over in theological education, with no presuppositions of any kind, we would hardly try to train men for a ministry in the world by first separating them completely from that world.[2]

Everything that has been said about the nature of the church, that is, its relationship to the triune God, mutual relationships within its fellowship, and its relationship to the world, can be summed up very well by a New Testament phrase, the "body of Christ." The body belongs to Christ, and by implication to his Father and to the Holy Spirit. The body has many members with interdependent responsibilities, and Paul speaks extensively of these in I Corinthians 12. The body is the means of expression outward to the world. It is the carrier of the personality of the individual. Therefore, when we use the term the body of Christ, we are, in effect, talking about this three-fold relationship which defines the nature of the church. Even where the term "body of Christ" is not used, these foundational truths about the church are assumed.

The nature of the church is closely related to the ministry of the church. At the bottom of the chart on page 23 you will notice the words: ministry to God, worship; ministry to the church, edification; and ministry to the world, witness and evangelism.[3] These are the objects of a theological training program, because these reflect the nature of the church. The church expresses its relationship to God by worship. Because the church is a family with mutual relationships, the need exists for a ministry of edification. Since the church is in the world it has a ministry to the world, expressed in verbal witness and in loving service.

This three-fold ministry is to be exercised in a general way by all of the members of the church. However, God has equipped some to exercise a unique leadership role. We may say that they have a special office. They both do their specific work and also train the general membership of the church to fulfill their ministry. Whether it be the general responsibility of worship, edification, and witness, or whether it be the special responsibility on a leadership level to lead and direct in worship, edification and witness, both of these levels of ministries are under the supreme authority and guidance of Jesus Christ, the Head of the church.

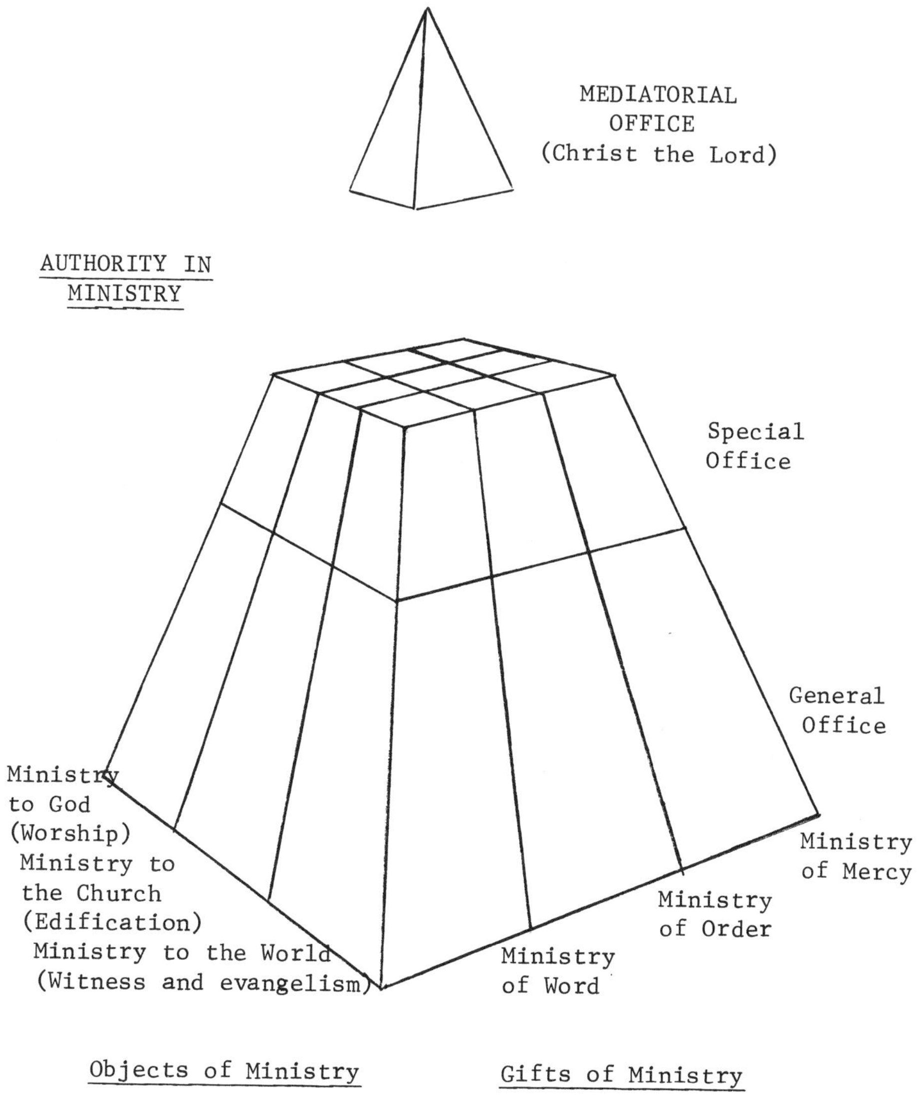

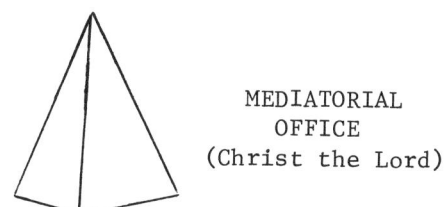

STRUCTURE OF ORDERED MINISTRY OF THE CHURCH

Chart by Edmund Clowney

NOTES FOR CHAPTER 2

1. Charles Dodd, <u>The Apostolic Preaching and Its Developments</u>, New York, Harper, 1936, p. 26.

2. James Hopewell, "Mission and Seminary Structure," *International Review of Missions*, Vol. 56 (April, 1967), p. 158.

3. This chart on the structure of the ordered ministry of the church was prepared by Dr. Edmund Clowney, President of Westminster Theological Seminary.

3
HOW GOD MAKES MINISTERS

It has already been mentioned that the question which should be asked prior to establishing any institution designed to train the ministry is: *whom* do we teach?

It has also been mentioned that our seminaries and Bible institutes do not *make* leaders, but rather they *train* leaders whom God has already made. To understand how God makes the leaders whom we should be training, we need to analyze the biblical teaching on the matter. It revolves basically around the concept of spiritual gifts.

I Corinthians 12:1 says, "Now concerning spiritual gifts, brethren, I would not have you ignorant." Ignorance of spiritual gifts is a dangerous sin of omission for anyone involved in theological education. It is surprising, however, to learn how many Christians who have given their lives to training the ministry hold very superficial views on spiritual gifts.

The opposite of ignorance is knowledge. God wants us to have a thorough knowledge of spiritual gifts, particularly if we are engaged in developing these gifts. First of all, we need a knowledge of the theory, or better yet the theology, of spiritual gifts. Secondly, we need a personal knowledge of what spiritual gifts we ourselves have. Relatively few Christians, including some seminary professors, have taken the time and effort necessary to discover their own gifts. Some don't even realize they have a gift at all! They are surprised when they are told that I Corinthians 12:7, "the manifestation of the Spirit is given to every man," applies to them personally.

Part of our trouble begins in the pulpit. Few churches in the U.S.A. emphasize the spiritual gifts as does, for example, the Peninsula Bible Church of Palo Alto, California. They have even developed a new slogan: "body-life evangelism." This is undoubtedly one reason why this is one of the most active and fastest-growing churches in the country. A deep hunger for more teaching concerning spiritual gifts may be part of the reason why the charismatic movement is enjoying so much success on a pandenominational level.

Before we identify the spiritual gifts specifically, we need to make two contrasts. First, spiritual gifts are not the same as natural talents. While there might be a close relationship between the two in some cases, they are widely separated in others. Natural talents are abilities which to one degree or another every member of the human race possesses. Spiritual gifts are supernatural endowments which God himself gives to a person when he becomes a Christian and thus enters as a functioning member of the body of Christ. In some instances, such as the gift of teaching for example, the natural talent which a person has before becoming a Christian may well be the spiritual gift he receives in the body of Christ. On the other hand, when it comes to such gifts as prophecy or tongues, the chances that these would carry over from some natural talent that a person might have had are very slim indeed.

The second important contrast is between spiritual gifts and spiritual fruit. The fruit of the Spirit is listed in Galatians 5:22: love, joy, peace, and the rest. Some err by speaking of "the gift of love," when love really is the fruit of the Spirit. The basic difference is that whereas only certain members of the body of Christ are expected to have a particular gift, such as the gift of pastor for example, all members of the body are expected to have the fruit. This is one reason why, right in the middle of the key scriptural passage on gifts (I Corinthians 12-14), the chapter on love, the fruit, is included as "the more excellent way." The first three verses of I Corinthians 13 contrast many different gifts (tongues, prophecy, wisdom, knowledge, faith, etc.) with the fruit. Spiritual fruit is a *sine qua non* for an effective use of spiritual gifts, but the two are distinct works of the Holy Spirit. Whereas there is a close relationship between a person's sanctification and the spiritual fruit characteristic of his life, there is no such relationship between sanctification and the spiritual gifts he possesses. The Corinthians are the best example of the latter. They had all the gifts (I Corinthians 1:7), but were among the most carnal brethren described in the New Testament.

Three key passages list the spiritual gifts in the body of Christ: I Corinthians 12, Romans 12, and Ephesians 4.

Granting one or two possible discrepancies in exegesis, if you correlate all the gifts in those passages, and add I Corinthians 7:7 and I Corinthians 13:3, you come out with a list something like this: apostleship, prophecy, teaching, evangelism, pastor, ministry, administration, wisdom, knowledge, faith, exhortation, miracles, healing, tongues, interpretation of tongues, discerning of spirits, giving, mercy, celibacy, and martyrdom.

No other specific gifts are mentioned in the New Testament, but the very fact that none of the individual lists is exhaustive would lead us to think that there may be others. What they might be, I do not know, but the possibility is open. Most Christians I know who have given adequate attention to spiritual gifts can locate theirs somewhere in the list we have made. Some may have one gift, some may have more than one.

Paul's choice of the human body as an illustration was a very happy one. Understanding what he means does not depend on coming from a particular culture or having a certain level of education. Everyone has at least an elementary understanding of the body. The body as an illustration is given in all three of the major passages on gifts mentioned above. What are some of the lessons learned here?

As the human body is made up of a large number of diverse members, so is the body of Christ. The reason for the diversity is unknown. What we do know is that the Spirit places the gifts in the members "as He will" (I Corinthians 12:11). The mystery of the diversity of gifts is parallel to the mystery of cell differentiation in the human body. Cell *division* in biology is well known and understood. Cell *differentiation*, or the process by which from one cell others divide off to form a kidney and others to form an eyeball, remains unknown to modern science. In the body of Christ, God entrusts his children with cell *division*--bringing new members into the body through evangelism (Romans 10:13-15). But he does not entrust them with *differentiation*, the awarding of spiritual gifts to his children; he reserves this for himself alone (I Corinthians 12:18).

No church in the world is without gifts if it is a truly Christian church. Christ promised: "I will build my church" (Matthew 16:18), and as I Corinthians 12 tells us, one of the ways he accomplishes this is to distribute the spiritual gifts. Not even a theological seminary has the power or authority to award a spiritual gift.

In spite of the great diversity of gifts, they are all coordinated under one head, both in the human body and in the body of Christ. No Christian can use his gift or gifts independently of the other Christians around him. No member of our human body could function properly if it were not connected organically to the head. Every member is to some degree dependent upon every other member. This is why "the eye cannot say to the hand, I have no need of you" (I Corinthians 12:21). Granted, some members of the body may be more beautiful than others. Lovers look at each other's eyes--not at their feet! But if the whole body were an eye, it would then be grotesque and ugly, no longer beautiful. To have three or four eyes would also detract from, not add to, their beauty. We can trust God, who fashioned the human body so perfectly, to fashion the body of Christ in the same way.

What does this mean for us?

Romans 12 tells us to present our bodies a living sacrifice to God. In order to do this, we must be "transformed" and "prove what is that good, and acceptable, and perfect will of God" (Romans 12:1-2). We must not make the mistake of isolating these verses from the total context of spiritual gifts in Romans 12, because one will only know the will of God for his life in a full way if he understands what spiritual gifts he has and what he is expected to do with them.

One of the features of this understanding is to be content with the gifts God gives to each one of us. Each Christian is to evaluate himself "soberly, according as God hath dealt to every man the measure of faith" (Romans 12:3). At the same time we should be content with what God has *not* given us, for a Christian should "not think of himself more highly than he ought to think" (Romans 12:3). The only way accurately to evaluate one's own responsibility before God is to recognize his spiritual gifts (Romans 12:6).

Perhaps all do not have as prolonged an experience as I had in this process. During my entire first term as a missionary, for example, I was disturbed and frustrated because I did not see substantial results from my evangelistic efforts, public or personal. I wanted to be another Billy Graham. I did not discount the possibility of a spiritual obstacle, but after much prayer and heart searching I could not discover one. Finally God brought me to the realization that I did not have the gift of an evangelist, and it was like a great burden being lifted off my back. I now know that God is not going to hold me responsible for the gift of evangelist at the judgment day because he didn't give it to me in the first place. I would still love to have the evangelistic power of Billy Graham, but I am no longer frustrated because I do not have it. I have come to a similar conclusion concerning the gift of pastor and other gifts.

At the same time, I now am quite aware that God has given me the gifts of teaching and administration. I feel I must dedicate my time and effort to developing and using these gifts, because I will have to give account for my stewardship over them some day.

This personal process of realistically evaluating one's exact place in the body of Christ yields three spiritual advantages. It reduces the possibility of false pride, since one realizes he has nothing to do with the fact that certain gifts have been bestowed upon him by God. It eliminates the type of false humility that says, "I can't do anything in my church--I don't have what it takes." And it prevents the envy that can so easily creep into the human heart because someone else might have a more beautiful or spectacular gift than I have.

Now, what does all this have to do with the extension seminary?

Possessing a spiritual gift and recognizing it is only the first step. From there on, a Christian is responsible for developing it. Paul wrote to Timothy to "stir up the gift of God which is in thee" (II Timothy 1:6).

In a very broad sense, this applies to every member of the body of Christ and the gifts he possesses. In a special sense, however, this refers to gifts of leadership in the church, or what we often call gifts of "ministry." Basically (although no absolute line can be drawn), the gifts of ministry are grouped in Ephesians 4:11. They would include apostleship, prophecy, evangelism, pastor, and teacher--maybe more from the other lists, although the details are not important at this juncture. What is important is that these special gifts are recognized publicly by the church by the laying on of hands. Paul speaks of Timothy's gift as "by the putting on of my hands," (II Timothy 1:6), and "with the laying on of the hands of the presbytery" (I Timothy 4:14). Paul even refers to himself in this specialized sense by saying that "God put me into the ministry" (I Timothy 1:12).

At this point a helpful distinction can be made between what we might call "theological education" and "Christian education." Whereas Christian education involves the edification of the entire body of Christ, the training of every Christian; theological education is more specialized, referring primarily to the training of the leadership of the Church.

It is the task of theological education to locate the persons to whom God has given these specialized gifts of the ministry, and assist them to develop their gifts to the highest degree possible. The specific objective is to provide them the training that will allow them to meet whatever requirement their church or denomination has established for public recognition as a minister. This is usually called ordination, but not always. Some churches with a lower view of the ordained ministry, such as the Plymouth Brethren, will ordain a large quantity of elders and not distinguish a professional pastor from the other elders. Other churches, such as the Anglican, place much higher formal requirements on the candidate for ordination. Sometimes ordination is symbolized by the use of the title "Reverend," sometimes "pastor" indicates functional ordination, and a wide variation of these definitions can be found in different ecclesiastical groups.

Theological education is not concerned with the way a given denomination publicly recognizes its ministry. It is concerned with preparing those whom God has called to this ministry, helping them meet whatever their church's standards might be. Theological education fails to the degree that it excludes gifted men and women who should be preparing themselves for their church's ministry.

The starting point for any program of theological education should be the *person* whom God has gifted for the ministry. This person-centeredness unfortunately has not been generally characteristic of many of our seminaries and Bible institutes in the past. The very structure of our institutions has excluded many of the men who have proven that they are gifted, while they include large quantities of young people who may wish they were gifted or who hope they might be gifted some day, but who have not yet been accepted by their churches as legitimate leaders. Melvin Hodges puts it very well when he says: "It is important that the missionary shall not limit his leadership training to the bright young men who at first glance would appear to be the best material. This is one of the fundamental errors of modern missions. The missionary has failed to see the importance of making place for mature men--the "elders" of the New Testament. Instead, he has gathered around him a group of the brightest minds, usually boys from the Mission School or children of converts, to give them special instruction."[1]

If we base our leadership training on spiritual gifts which have been tried and proven, we will find that the majority of our students are mature men with homes, families, jobs, and community responsibilities. This is a description which does not too well fit the typical student whom most of us have been training through the years. It *does* fit I Timothy 3:1-7.

One of the most difficult problems for those who are being initiated into the principles of the extension seminary is to conjure up the proper mental image when the word "student" is mentioned. "We must train our young people for the ministry," is uppermost in our minds, when in many cases the grandfather, not the young person, is the one who has been gifted, and therefore called, and who needs the training. An excellent analysis of this situation by Ross Kinsler bears repeating here: "This is not simply a matter of mobilizing the layman. It is also a question of leadership. Technical studies (and common sense) indicate that the present system of theological training and ordination is ineffectual in the selection and development of leaders. On the one hand, the seminaries are set up for men and women who are young, just out of college, and who have had almost no chance to prove themselves in the world or even to develop their gifts in the church . . . On the other hand those men and women who do prove themselves in the world and gain experience and earn positions of leadership in the organizations of the church find it almost impossible to go to seminary, and must always sit under the tutelage of the former group.[2]

Confusion as to the "call to the ministry" is one of the roots of the problem. The self-assertion that a person has received a mystical call to the ministry should not be sufficient for seminary admission. The confirmation of the church, such as took place in the case of Barnabas and Saul in Acts 13:1-3, is equally necessary. But responsible churches will only confirm a call when sufficient evidence of possessing the spiritual gift has been accumulated. This, almost invariably, implies a spiritual, social, psychological, and physical maturity which we have not insisted on to any great extent in the past. Receiving the spiritual gift of pastor, for example, must not be distinguished from the call to the pastorate. When the church recognizes that a person has the gift of pastor they *ipso facto* confirm his call to the pastorate.

Many theological educators, especially those who are now involved in extension seminary programs, admit that much time and money has been invested in training good people, but people who after all had not been gifted by God for the ministry. Of course, there are many outstanding exceptions to this. Thousands of today's effective church leaders have been trained in traditional institutions. But this is not the point we are making here. While we are pleased with those who *have* been trained, we are pointing out that we have not been sufficiently concerned with those who *have not* or *are not* being trained. As has been mentioned before, the good that our traditional system is doing should be preserved and continued, but the challenge of doing even better should be accepted and acted upon.

The theological basis for this challenge, therefore, is the New Testament teaching on spiritual gifts. Basing ministerial training on gifted men will force our training schools to become more person-centered and thus help us in the process of humanizing theological education.

"Concerning spiritual gifts, brethren, I would not have you ignorant" (I Corinthians 12:1).

NOTES FOR CHAPTER 3

1. Melvin L. Hodges, "The Selection of Ministerial Candidates," *Church Growth Bulletin Volumes I-V*, Donald A. McGavran, ed., South Pasadena, William Carey Library, 1969, p. 232.

2. F. Ross Kinsler, "Extend the Seminaries," Theological Education by Extension, Ralph D. Winter, ed., South Pasadena, William Carey Library, 1969, pp. 246-247.

4
JESUS, THE MODEL TEACHER

The Gospel records indicate that Jesus Christ was an outstanding teacher. He was called a *teacher* by his disciples, by his opponents, and by the people in general. Furthermore, all the Gospels except Luke use the Aramaic Rabbi or its equivalent Rabboni, which also means "teacher."

The New Testament presents Jesus as a teacher who is both different from and similar to other teachers of that period.[1] In common with other teachers or rabbis, he had disciples. With the Gospel writers, the term "disciple" had a wider meaning than in its normal usage. For example, the "people of the land," sinners, and publicans were called disciples. At least 90 percent of the 230 usages of the term "disciple" in the New Testament are not limited to the Twelve.

Jesus was different from other rabbis in the first century in that he did not establish a formal school for the teaching of his disciples. In common with others rabbis, he had a definite content to impart, but he claimed that his teaching was directly from God. He did not depend on the authority of a particular school nor upon the ordination of an important rabbi for its validity. He taught his disciples important truths, but the crux of all his doctrine was that his disciples should be committed to him as a person.

The verb *didasko*, meaning to teach, is often used to describe Jesus' activity. It is usually not followed by an object, that is, there is not as much emphasis upon what he taught as upon the one who was doing the teaching.[2] Thus, the most important aspect of His teaching was that the disciples would recognize him for who he was and give themselves to him in a commitment of faith.

Jesus, the Model Teacher

In common with other teachers of that period, Jesus was questioned on his doctrine and upon his conduct. Those who would trip him up asked him about paying tribute to Caesar, about the resurrection from the dead, and about the doctrine of marriage and divorce. It was common for disciples in that period to serve their rabbis in the menial affairs of life, a practice also true of Jesus' disciples. They brought his sandals, prepared the road before him, procured a donkey for his use, rowed the boats from which he taught, and distributed food to the multitudes.

It is instructive to read the Gospels with the precise goal of trying to understand how Jesus taught, as well as who he taught and what he taught. The concern of this chapter is to emphasize *how* Jesus taught and to note the potential relationship of these techniques to the concepts of theological education by extension.

First of all, Jesus taught by example.[3] Luke records, "Jesus was praying in a certain place and when he ceased, one of his disciples said to him, Lord, teach us to pray, as John taught his disciple" (Luke 11:1). The best type of teaching will stimulate questions and will motivate and arouse curiosity on the part of the learner.

On another occasion, Jesus left his disciples a similar example of prayer (Mark 1:35-39). This event is one of a series illustrating for us a typically busy day in the life of Jesus Christ. His activities commenced early in the morning at the synagogue in Capernaum. While he was teaching, a man possessed by an evil spirit stood up and cried out, "What have you to do with us, Jesus of Nazareth. Have you come to destroy us? I know who you are, the Holy One of God," (Mark 1:24). After Jesus had cast out the evil spirit from this man, he left the synagogue and went to the house of Simon and Andrew. Here Simon Peter's mother-in-law was sick. After Jesus spent some time in this home healing her, he returned to the place where he was staying, and many who were sick or possessed by demons came to be healed. Although Jesus was busy dealing with the needs of these people until very late in the evening, he arose early the next day and went to pray in a lonely desert place. When the sun had risen, the crowds, who still had some unmet needs, came to the door and asked where Jesus was. Peter said that he did not know, but he went and found Jesus and reported to him, "Everyone is searching for you." Jesus, however, did not respond to this request in the way that Peter had hoped. Instead he said, "Let us go on to the next town that I might preach there also, for that is why I came out" (Mark 1:38).

This particular sequence of events, an unforgettable lesson on prayer, is recorded for us in all three Synoptic Gospels. When Jesus taught his disciples about prayer he did not do it with a formal lecture. We find no place in the four Gospels where Jesus sat down and gave his disciples a systematic lecture on the doctrine of prayer. Nevertheless, through occasions such as these recorded by Luke and Mark, Jesus taught his disciples a great deal about prayer. He taught them that it was important to pray even when very busy. He taught them the need to pray before important decisions. He taught them that prayer is an intimate experience with God. The term he used in prayer when addressing God was "Abba." This was not ordinarily used in prayer by Jewish religious leaders. They employed a more general name when speaking to God as Father. When Jesus prayed he used this extremely intimate term which best could be translated into English as "Daddy." Paul told the Christians at Rome that when the Holy Spirit comes into their heart they will cry, "Abba Father," (Romans 8:15). The early church learned how to use the word "Abba," and they learned the intimacy and reality of prayer because this is the way that Jesus himself prayed.[4]

Prayer is not the only subject which Jesus taught by example. Alexander Hay[5] has pointed out that there are ten essentials for the training of disciples illustrated from the life of Christ. He sought their spiritual development. He taught them how to evangelize, to know and use the scriptures, to have faith in God, to minister in the power of the Spirit. He led them to understand and appropriate the life and ministry of prayer in the Spirit, and to be absolutely obedient to the will of God. From him they learned to exercise unwavering faith, to love God and man, and to work together in dedication to God's will. In each of these areas it was his example, more than it was his systematized instruction, which enabled them to know what they ought to be and do.

Teaching by example helps to explain the authority of Christ--an authority which listeners claimed was far different from that possessed by other teachers at that time.[6] We may be tempted to say that Jesus Christ had this kind of authority, but that we cannot be like him. In one sense this is true and yet Paul exhorted, "You must imitate me, even as I imitate Christ" (I Corinthians 11:1). He did not say, "Keep your eyes upon Jesus only, and do not follow man." To some degree the Gospel had become incarnated in his life, for he also was teaching by example.

New Testament truth is truth with a body. It is not abstract doctrine of Greek philosophy, but it rather is truth

Jesus, the Model Teacher

which has entered into a living situation. This truth was the first century audio-visual. Thus it was that John could write, "That . . . which we have heard, which we have seen with our eyes . . . concerning the Word of life . . . we declare to you" (I John 1:1-2).

Some have suggested that teaching by example is more difficult in theological education by extension than it is in the traditional seminary program. The argument is that the limited time the teacher is able to spend with the pupil is not sufficient to be a good example. The validity of this criticism will depend upon the local situation and upon the teacher involved. If the teacher seeks to be efficient in the North American sense and spends only a minimal amount of time in the weekly meetings with the students this criticism will be true. However, if he utilizes the weekly relationship with his pupils to learn more about their homes, their families, and their work, possibly staying at the place of weekly meeting overnight, extension training affords a better opportunity to the teacher to be an example than would ordinarily be the case in a resident seminary program.

In the second place, Jesus Christ taught his disciples in living situations. With him there was no dichotomy of class and life. Every situation was real without any artificiality. Teaching was always relevant because the disciples were involved in the world. No necessity existed for Jesus periodically to make spot announcements about the need for his disciples to be relevant to the world. Jesus was teaching them on a grass root level. They themselves were aware of the need, because they were living in and through the situation with Christ.

When the disciples came down from the Mount of Transfiguration, they were confronted by a man with a particular problem. His son was possessed of an evil spirit who threw him into the fire and into the water. The disciples were unable to do anything for this afflicted young man. Later when Jesus came, he called for the father to bring his son to him. He rebuked the evil spirit, cast him out, and the boy was cured immediately. After the man and his son had gone away, the disciples came to Jesus and asked, "Lord, why could we not cast the demon out?" Jesus replied, "This kind does not come out except by prayer and by fasting" (Mark 9:29).

Suppose that Jesus had used a more traditional form of education. He might have given a lecture on the subject of evil spirits. He would have spoken first about evil spirits that can be expelled through prayer. The second point of this lecture would be that, in addition to prayer, there is frequent necessity to fast. The disciples would have taken copious notes on everything that Jesus had said about evil spirits—about the type that could be cast out by prayer, and about the type that demanded the use of fasting. When they left this classroom situation and went into the world, they would take their notebooks with them. Sooner or later, they would meet someone possessed of an evil spirit, at which time they would need to peruse their notebooks to find the needed material. Such learning would have been very artificial.

Jesus taught his disciples by proceeding from the known to the unknown. He started where they were. He utilized life situations around him which would enable him to gain their attention. For this reason, Jesus' parables have great teaching value. Think also of the expression, "the Gospel of the Kingdom," which Jesus often used when speaking about the Kingdom of God. This phrase has within it both that which is well known and that which is relatively unknown. The Jewish people to whom he was speaking understood the Old Testament teaching about the Kingdom. This concept had been perverted by the emphases of Judaism during the inter-biblical period, but first-century Hebrews still had some concept of the Kingdom. Jesus, however, spoke about the "Gospel of the Kingdom." In the Greek Old Testament, the verb which we translate "to evangelize" is found two or three times, but the noun "Gospel" is not used. This term and its concept is new, and Jesus could put into it the content he desired. By linking these two terms, the "Gospel" and the "Kingdom" he was talking at once about something which the people knew and about something which they did not know. In the same way, when he described himself as the Son of man, Jesus was using a concept that, at least, was vaguely familiar to people of his time. Although it is a phrase which we seldom use or incorrectly interpret, it was a term familiar to Jewish people at the time of Jesus' ministry.

In the fourth place, the teaching of Jesus was personalized. It was individualized in accordance with the need of the person to whom Jesus was speaking. Everyone has general needs. If we are talking about the Gospel of Christ, we recognize that each person is a sinner, that he needs to confess his sin, to trust Christ as his personal Savior, and to commit his way to Christ in a life of discipleship. People, however, not only have general needs, they also have specific needs. And the best teaching will relate itself in a particular way to the needs which people individually have. Think of Jesus' conversation with the rich young ruler. Here was a young man who asked him, "Good Teacher, what must I do to inherit eternal life?" Jesus reminded him of the commandments which he had long known. When the young man heard these statements, he protested that he had obeyed all these commandments from the time he was very young. Jesus then gave to him a specific commandment, "You lack one thing, go, sell what you have and give to the poor and you will have treasure in heaven. And come, take up the cross and follow me" (Mark 10:21).

As far as the New Testament record goes, Jesus did not place a similar demand upon any other person who came to him. This young man had a particular need. He could not follow Christ unless he had come to grips with what was the central sin of his life. Only if he had responded to Christ in terms of this basic problem would he truly have become a disciple. Our teaching and our preaching is often so general that it never gets behind the facade which people have erected as a barrier between themselves and God. We need to take the time to understand the needs, problems and difficulties which people have, and then to personalize our teaching in such a way that by the power of the Holy Spirit they are brought face to face with the specific demands of Christ upon them.

One of the difficulties in our traditional seminary program is that we lump together those of diverse educational and Christian backgrounds and expect to teach them all by utilizing the same methods and the same content. There is no provision, apart from counseling sessions, to make the educational process a personal and individual experience.

In the fifth place, Jesus Christ trained by evaluating people. This was a part of the learning process. When the seventy returned from the mission on which he had sent them, they were very happy because demons were subject to them in Christ's name. He quickly reminded them that the true cause for joy was never to be their own accomplishments, but rather what God had done for them. "Rejoice that your names are written in heaven" (Luke 10:20).

On another occasion, when they were sailing across the Sea of Galilee, Jesus and his disciples were involved in a tremendous storm. He noted their fear and asked, "Why are you fearful? Do you have no faith?" (Mark 4:40). At another time, he rebuked them even more sharply because they had forgotten the lesson of the feeding of the 5,000 and the feeding of the 4,000.

If we merely impart content to our students and do not take the time to know them, to understand them, and to live with them to the degree that we are able to evaluate them, we are not fully educating them. The traditional school does not afford us a good context in which to evaluate the total life of the student. We are able to tell how he does in his courses, how he is able to articulate, whether he does better on an objective test or on an essay test, and whether or not he turns assignments in on time. However, we often know little about many of those things that will cause him to succeed or fail in his ministry.

On evaluation forms sent to me by churches and by mission boards, the question with which I always have the most difficulty is, "How does this person handle his finances? What are his attitudes toward money?" Although this is a tremendously important matter, this is the question which I most frequently must leave unanswered. Seldom do I know a student well enough to evaluate his attitudes toward money.

Most seminaries have some type of procedure to evaluate the personality and the life of their students. Although these procedures may be stated very clearly, actual evaluation is one of the most difficult things for any school to implement. During the first and the second years, the faculty desire to give the student a bit more time to prove himself. By the third year they conclude that it would be a shame not to graduate him, since he has already studied for two years. Finally, they conclude that even though a student may possibly be a problem, "we will graduate him and let the churches correct his difficulties."

Theological education by extension affords a better context in which to evaluate the student. Those being trained are mature leaders already working in the church. They are educated in an environment closely related to the church. Therefore, the evaluation can easily be done by members of the church in which they are serving. This evaluation is much more complete, because the church is able to see the student in the total environment in which he is living.

Finally, Jesus taught his disciples by delegating important work to them. The best example of this is to be found in Matthew 28 when Jesus commits to his disciples the Great Commission. They were far from perfect at this time. In fact, Matthew records, "And when they saw him, they worshipped him, but some doubted," (28:17). It was to these doubting, fearful, imperfect disciples of his that Jesus gave the Great Commission. He had confidence that they would be able to carry out this "mission impossible." Nothing will help a student to learn faster or to seek to implement his teaching in a better way than to know that his teacher has confidence in him. Jesus not only gave them the command, he promised them his own presence and he promised them the direction and the power of the Holy Spirit.

The task of teaching around the world often is made more difficult because we do not seem to believe that what God the Holy Spirit has done in our lives, he is able also to do in the lives of those whom we teach. A notable exception to this pattern was found in Taiwan in the 1930's. Missionaries were concerned to preach the gospel to the various mountain tribes. The Japanese were ruling Taiwan at the time, and it was impossible for the missionaries themselves to go into these mountain areas. An aborigine woman by the name of Chi Wang was married to a Chinese Christian. As a result of going to church with her husband, she made a decision to follow Christ and joined a Presbyterian church on the east coast of Taiwan. Shortly after this time, Dr. James Dickson, a missionary with the Canadian Presbyterian board, heard of Chi Wang's conversion and made a trip to the east coast to see her. He suggested that she come with him to Bible school in the city of Tan Shui in northwestern Taiwan. From all appearances this was a ridiculous suggestion. Chi Wang was a woman in a man's culture. She was relatively old for that society and she did not have the prerequisite educational background for further study.

However, she went with Dr. Dickson and commenced her study. Going to school was very difficult for her. She was used to working long hours in her fields without becoming tired, but when she sat in hard chairs and listened to someone lecturing all day long, she confessed that she quickly became exhausted. Jim Dickson encouraged her in her studies and tried to help her in every way possible. After six months Chi Wang returned to her village on the east coast near Hwalien and led very simple study groups for some of her own people who came to her secretly from different mountain villages. After being instructed by Chi Wang and urged to go back and teach the Gospel, they went to several villages and sought to make Christ known in various ways.

The final result of what started in these years at the end of the 1930's can now be seen in Taiwan where the Presbyterian church has over 400 churches among the several aborigine groups and where nearly 70,000 out of 200,00 have put their faith in Christ. Would this movement ever have started if there had not been a missionary who believed that this woman, who, on the surface, had so little potential, was indeed able to be the key who could open the door for the entrance of the Gospel into the mountains of Taiwan?

Jesus Christ is the model teacher. He taught by example. He taught in living situations. He taught by proceeding from the known to the unknown. His teaching was personalized. As he taught he evaluated the lives of his students. He had confidence in them. He delegated important work to them. It was these disciples, these students who had learned under the model teacher, who took his Gospel to the ends of the Roman Empire.7

NOTES ON CHAPTER 4

1. Much of this material is from Rengstorf "Didasko" in Gerhard Kittel (ed.) Theological Dictionary of the New Testament, English Edition, Eerdman, 1964. Volume II, pp. 138-143.

   See also W. D. Davies, The Setting of the Sermon on the Mount, Cambridge, 1964, pp. 418-419, 422-425.

2. Rengstorf, "Didasko," p. 141.

3. I am indebted to Dr. Howard Hendricks of Dallas Theological Seminary for the general outline of this chapter.

4. Joachim Jeremias, The Prayers of Jesus, Napervile, Allenson, Inc., 1967, Chapter 1, "Abba," pp. 11-65.

5. Alexander Hay, The New Testament Order for Church and Missionary, Buenes Aires, Argentina, New Testament Missionary Union, 1947, Supplement to Chapter IV.

6. David Daube, The New Testament and Rabbinic Judaism, London University of London, 1956, pp. 206, 16.

   He suggests the implication of this question is, "How is it you have authority as an ordained teacher and not as the unlearned teachers?" Even if corrent, this interpretation says nothing about the ultimate source of Jesus' teaching.

7. Books of value on Jesus as a teacher are:

   A. B. Bruce, The Training of the Twelve, Edinburgh, T. & T. Clark, 1908.

   Robert E. Coleman, The Master Plan of Evangelism, New York, Revell, 1964.

   H. H. Horne, Jesus the Master Teacher, Grand Rapids, Kregel, 1968.

5

WHY PAUL WAS SUCCESSFUL IN TEACHING

Teaching was central in the ministry of the Apostle Paul. He considered himself a teacher (II Timothy 1:11, I Timothy 2:7; Galatians 1:28), and he also was careful to urge this ministry upon those for whom he was responsible. Throughout the Pastoral epistles we constantly see this exhortation to teach (I Timothy 4:11; 6:2; II Timothy 2:2). Paul clearly recognized the importance of teaching in the lives of these who were his colleagues in making Christ known.

Not only did Paul believe that he and his fellow-workers had been called to teach, he also saw teaching as a responsibility of all Christians. He exhorted the Colossian Christians to "Let the word of Christ dwell in you richly as you teach and admonish one another in all wisdom . . . , "(Colossians 3:16). Here again we see that those gifts of the Holy Spirit given to the leadership level of the church for ministry are shared in some measure by all Christians. A truth often neglected in the body of Christ is that every believer should teach God's Word to other members of the Christian family.

Paul used a variety of methods in his teaching ministry. These can be understood by noting the terms Luke uses to describe his teaching. Paul stayed a year and six months in Corinth (Acts 18:11) *teaching* (*didasko*) the word of God among them. *Didasko* implies "to reduce a subject to its simplest essentials, to analyze it point by point, to fix its meaning by positive and negative definition, to show how each part links with the rest--and to go on explaining" until the hearers have grasped it.[1] It is no mere once-for-all proclamation under the assumption that once I have said it, the learner certainly has learned it. Rather is it an explanation and a communication of truth in a variety of ways until the learner has comprehended what is involved.

Dr. Arthur Glasser tells of going into a rural area in China to do itinerant evangelism. In one particular village there was a man who had repeatedly heard him explain the Gospel. Every time that Dr. Glasser went through this village he sought out this man and explained the message to him. It appeared that he understood what was being said. After a year of making these repeated contacts, Dr. Glasser saw him again, and once more taught the message of Christ to him. On this occasion the man said, "Oh, is that what you mean? I see it now." Even though he had heard the truth about Christ many times, only now was it clear to him.

So often we think that evangelism or preaching occurs previous to the point of decision and that Christian education begins only after a person has received Christ. With Paul, however, Christian education in its broadest sense was a part of his evangelistic ministry. He understood that one of the best ays, if not the best way, to preach the Gospel is by teaching.

Another word used by Luke to describe Paul's teaching ministry is the verb translated "to dispute" (Acts 9:28). In the course of presenting the message of Christ, Paul occasionally entered into a process of argumentation with people. He not only spoke, but he allowed his listeners to speak. He sought to understand their point of view at the same time that he was presenting his perspective. He was teaching the gospel by a process of dialogue.

Luke records also that Paul "argued in the synagogue every Sabbath" (Acts 18:4; 19:8). This was not a monologue, a lecture, or one-way communication. Paul was ready to allow the receptor of his communication to give him feedback that then enabled him to clarify the truth he was presenting. This two-way communication process does not mean that Paul was deficient in his convictions, because along with the verbs "argue," or "reason," Luke records that Paul "persuaded" Jews and Greeks about the Kingdom of God (Acts 18:4; 19:8). Paul did not teach truth abstractly. He would not have fallen into the error of those who frequently say, "It is my responsibility to teach and God will give the results." Paul knew that he himself had an obligation to persuade. He had a burden not only to make Christ known but, by the power of the Holy Spirit, to seek to lead men to a decision for Christ. His was not a disinterested communication. He pled with men to be reconciled to God (II Corinthians 5:20).

A second thing to be noted about Paul's principles of teaching is that he believed he had a definite message to be communicated. He frequently uses the word "tradition," either in its verbal or noun form (I Corinthians 15:3; II Timothy 2:2). This tradition had a definite doctrinal content. In the I Corinthians 15:3 formulation it included the death, burial and resurrection of Jesus Christ. The apostolic tradition also provided ethical exhortation for the early church.[2] Paul commands Christians at Thessalonica to "keep away from any brother who is living in idleness and not in accord with the tradition that you received from us" (II Thessalonians 3:16).

The source of the doctrinal or ethical tradition used by Paul was at least three-fold. First of all was the Old Testament. Early believers apparently had available to them an informal oral or written tradition of Old Testament quotations commonly used by the church. Paul also made extensive use of the words of Jesus. He seldom quoted Jesus verbatim, but frequently alluded to his words. One German scholar has noted nearly 1,000 allusions to the words of Jesus in the teaching of Paul.[3]

A third source of the tradition that Paul had received was the informal or even more formal teaching materials used by the early church. Whether the Old Testament, the words of Jesus, or these early teaching materials, Paul was clear that the ultimate source of that which he had received and for which he was responsible was God himself.[4]

Despite the fact that Paul knew he was passing on a definite content, two factors guided his presentation. In the first place, Paul was clear that his goal was not merely to impart knowledge but to teach obedience. The end point of his teaching process was not to evaluate how much the learner was able to memorize or to repeat back to him. The basic question was, "Is this truth lived out now in your life in obedience?" In his relationship with the Corinthian church, Paul reminds them that he is sending "Timothy, my beloved and faithful child in the Lord, to remind you of my ways in Christ, as I teach them everywhere in every church" (I Corinthians 4:17). He then goes on to point out that "my ways in Christ" are to be obeyed, because "the Kingdom of God does not consist in talk but in power" (I Corinthians 4:20). The same emphasis on obedience is seen in the Great Commission where Jesus commands his disciples "go therefore and make disciples of all nations, . . . teaching them to *observe* all that I have commanded you" (Matthew 28:19-20). The aim of their teaching was not to impart knowledge but to produce obedient disciples.

In my contact with the Taroko tribe in Taiwan, I have often been impressed with how little they know but how well they obey what they know. At the beginning of their movement

toward Christ they really knew only three truths. They were
sure God loved them and that he had sent his Son to die for
their sins. In the second place, they knew that a Christian
must suffer persecution when he believed. Thirdly, they knew
the power and the priority of prayer. From our sophisticated
viewpoint these may not appear to be profound truths. However,
because of this thorough obedience God poured out such a blessing upon the mountain peoples of Taiwan that one out of every
three believed in Christ in a movement that has been called the
"Pentecost of the Hills."

Paul also changed the form of his message to suit the differing audiences to which he was speaking. In the record of
Acts 13, he speaks to a congregation of Jewish people. In the
following chapter Luke describes his approach to a group of
very superstitious and idolatrous Gentiles. On Mars Hill
(Acts 17) Paul is again speaking to those immersed in idolatry
and superstition, but these are intellectual leaders in the
city of Athens. In each instance the Gospel content assumes a
different shape. The central core of the message is the same,
but Paul does not communicate it to the people in the same way.

We have been very negligent in this matter. Uncritically,
we have said the Gospel is the same for all people. By this we
correctly mean that all men are alienated from God, that they
need a Saviour, and that they are saved by putting their trust
in Jesus Christ, the crucified, buried, resurrected and ascended Saviour. These are eternal truths, but the ways in
which we present them, those things which we are going to emphasize and the ways in which we will relate this truth to what
the people already know are going to be different in each separate situation. If we neglect the fact that our receptor is
not the same in differing situations, we will not communicate
the Gospel in the way that Paul did it.

Unfortunately, missionaries are not always able to relate
well to the culture in which they are working. An American anthropologist spent a summer recently in a country in Southeast
Asia analyzing certain aspects of this culture. During the
course of his stay there he had frequent opportunities to speak
with missionaries. His conclusions were not encouraging. He
reported, "In my conversations with missionaries, I did not
find one who understood the culture as a whole. Perhaps some
of them understood bits and pieces of it, but none seemed to
understand either that the bits and pieces were part of one
whole or that they related to each other." "This, " he continued, "did not bother me. Missionaries are busy people, and if
they did not know these things perhaps they could be excused.
More important, however," he said, "I did not meet any

missionary who even thought it was important to know these things." If this is indeed our approach to culture--a feeling that culture is unimportant or that it is our enemy--how then can we imitate the Apostle Paul in this teaching principle? The first requisite for good teaching is that we must understand our target, the receptor of the communication, the one whom we are trying to teach.

In the third place, Paul was selective in his training process. He exhorted Timothy, "The things which you have heard from me from among many witnesses, the same commit to faithful men who will be able to teach others also" (II Timothy 2:2). Paul had a team of men who worked with him. These men were gifted, not necessarily because of a natural talent, but because they had received gifts of the Holy Spirit which enabled them to teach. Their call had been verified by their gifts.

They were faithful from the negative standpoint because they loyally guarded the tradition which they had received. Positively, they were committed to passing on this tradition. It would not stop with them. They were able to teach others because of their gifts, and they were ready to teach others because they were committed, faithful men.

A common problem in all of our training schools is that we have very young people coming to us who, when they are questioned as to their reasons for wanting to study, will usually say, "I have been called to serve God." We are not as careful as we ought to be to seek concrete evidence that they have gifts which would prepare them for the ministry and which would validate their calling.

Paul taught his team in a variety of ways. They traveled with him and saw the way in which he worked. He gave them responsibilities to fulfill. He delegated them to go and visit churches where they had previously worked together as a team. Paul carried books with him, and, undoubtedly, used some of these books as a means of teaching his team. His ways in Christ were known to them (I Corinthians 4:17), and this apprenticeship type of training prepared them to fulfill the ministry which God had given them in the churches.

In the fourth place, Christ was the center of the content which Paul taught in the churches. He exhorted the Christians at Ephesus, "You did not so learn Christ assuming that you had heard about him and were taught in him as the truth is in Jesus. Put off your old nature which belongs to your former manner of life and is corrupt through deceitful lusts and be renewed in the spirit of your mind and put on the new nature created after the likeness of God in true righteousness and holiness" (Ephesians 4:22-24). Christ is the content and goal of the teaching, and, in reality, Christ himself, by the Holy Spirit, is teaching through Paul. The end product of Paul's teaching was that the learner might be like Jesus Christ.

Here is a solid foundation for an indigenous theology. We are not merely teaching a factual content much of which may have accretions developed within our North American culture. We are not merely teaching Christ as he has been understood by our sending churches. We are not merely going through a stereotyped process of using human methodology, techniques, and resources to teach. Rather we are presenting the Christ of God's unique revelation. He is freed from the specific cultural baggage which has developed about his person in our society. He will become incarnate, as it were, in the target culture. In this way, we will have what we can call Indian Christians, African Christians and Chinese Christians. These believers will not necessarily think alike, feel alike, or act alike. They will have their own personal relationship to Jesus Christ which will express itself uniquely in the culture where they are.

This does not mean that their faith will not have common elements with the faith of Christians in other countries. Yes, it certainly will have. A Christian is a Christian because of his relationship to the Christ presented in God's Word. This, however, is far different from saying that a Chinese Christian must think and feel and act in the same way as an American Christian does.

The world is filled with an abundance of excellent ethical systems. If we who teach the Christian faith do not make it very clear that the uniqueness of Christianity is in the person of Jesus Christ himself, the world will wrongly read us to understand that the Christian message is only one more system of morality.

Finally, Paul taught principles and not specific details. The best example of this is the first Corinthian epistle. This church had many problems, and they came to Paul to seek solutions. He answered them by enunciating principles that could answer their current problems and give guidelines to solve future difficulties. Paul had great confidence in the Holy Spirit to interpret the principles of the Christian life in the believers' experiences.

Roland Allen is well known for his book, _Missionary Methods, St. Paul's or Ours_. Another book written by him that has not been so widely acclaimed is _The Spontaneous Expansion_ of the Church. Here Allen argues persuasively that Paul did not hedge his churches about with minute details and regulations to predetermine everything they should do. He committed the principles of God's Word to them, encouraged them to trust the Holy Spirit, and taught them to develop their own life in an indigenous manner fitting to the environment in which they were living. The result of this approach? Instant indigenous church.[5]

Our task, therefore, in teaching is to give people the principles of God's word and some examples on how to apply these principles in concrete, life situations. Furthermore, we must reserve immediate judgment on questionable issues, allow the Holy Spirit freedom to direct and believe that God is able to work in their lives even as he has worked in ours.

In theological education we cannot proceed on the supposition that during the time a student is in school we must teach him everything he needs to know about the Word of God, pastoral theology, church history, and the planting of churches. During his formal school experience we are giving him the tools that will help him in his life-long, permanent study of the Word of God. We are teaching him principles of action from God's Word. We are exhorting him to develop attitudes he will need in his work.

Students everywhere have a tendency to depend upon rote memory--a learning process crucial to many indigenous educational systems around the world. Why is this? At least a portion of the blame for stress upon memory is that we ourselves are so content-oriented in our approach that the students are merely responding to the way we teach. An emphasis upon utilizing principles to teach students how to think may help to break this vicious cycle.

In conclusion, Paul was not stereotyped in his teaching. He used a variety of techniques. Although he recognized that there was a definite content to be taught, he did not present facts as an end in themselves, but as a means to lead the learner to obedience. Moreover, he communicated this content differently for each audience he was speaking to. Paul did not feel that everyone could be a teacher on the church leadership level. Therefore, he evaluated carefully who had gifts of the Holy Spirit for teaching and concentrated his efforts on them. His teaching centered upon Jesus Christ. He taught people to discover the principles of God's Word, and then he helped them as they tried to apply these truths to living situations.[6]

NOTES FOR CHAPTER 5

1. J. I. Packer, Evangelism and the Sovereignty of God, Chicago: IVCF Press, 1961, p. 48.

2. Ian Muirhead, Education in the New Testament, New York: Association Press, 1965, Chapter 3, pp. 49-64.

3. Otto Roller, Das Formular Der Paulinischen Briefe, Stuggart: W. Kohlhammer, 1933.

4. For a concise treatment of the source of Paul's tradition see Archibald Hunter, Paul and His Predecessors, (Rev. ed.), Philadelphia: Westminster Press, 1961.

5. Allen develops this thesis also in Chapter 4, "St. Paul and the Judaizers: A Dialogue" in his book, The Ministry of the Spirit, Grand Rapids: Eerdmans, 1962.

6. A classic book helpful in any consideration of Paul as a teacher is Howard T. Kuist, The Pedagogy of Paul, George H. Doran Company, 1925.

6
FORMS OF THEOLOGICAL EDUCATION THROUGH HISTORY

The past has a great future. Much can be learned by briefly examining the history of theological education. Not only are we helped to avoid the mistakes of the past, but we will derive comfort in learning that current problems were faced by other generations. They, too, struggled with the dichotomy of the clergy and laity, saw the need for a ministry on various academic levels, sought to resolve the tension between theory and practice, and emphasized the need for tutorial as well as formal training.

Our present pattern of theological education is a relative newcomer on the scene of ministerial training. It cannot be absolutized as the "Biblical" way of training people--the only way that God has given to his church. Little value, then, will come by uncritically exporting it as a pattern for overseas churches. Rather, we should encourage them to see how the Holy Spirit can help in developing an education more functional to their own environment and their needs.

Form in theological education must be separated from the function or purpose of the church in any given age or environment. The church has always developed a variety of forms to fulfill its God-given function of training leaders to meet specific needs. This function is clearly rooted in the Scripture. But there is no one Biblical form by which this function must be carried out. A particular form is useful and worthy to be perpetuated only as it is a vehicle for meeting the ministerial needs that the church has. When it is dysfunctional, it can only be discarded.

Many missionaries, unfortunately, have frequently confused form and function. Their experience in the lands from which they come has introduced them to one or more forms of theological education. These forms have been relatively efficient in meeting the needs of an affluent, but rather static church with well established norms for ministry. The problem has come when these forms used in North America, Great Britain and the Continent have been transplanted into an overseas environment where the ministerial function has been far different.

NEW TESTAMENT PERIOD TO THE REFORMATION

The church has always had some form of training for its leaders. In the New Testament period there were no formal theological schools. The disciples of Jesus learned by being with him (Mark 3:13-19). They apparently had general knowledge equal to that of their peers, but, lacking formal education, they were accused of being "uneducated, common men" (Acts 4:13). Paul received a classical training at the University of Tarsus and a rabbinic education in Jerusalem.

Paul followed the apprentice method of Jesus in training a company of men who travelled with him. Carefully selected by him during his missionary journeys, these men were trained "on the job" in the truths of Scripture, and perhaps in the knowledge common to the men among whom they worked. And Paul, in turn, expected Timothy and others to train faithful men of proven teaching ability who would be continuing links in this educational chain.

Vast geographical areas needed to be conquered for Christ during this era. Consequently, great stress was placed upon a lay leadership which quickly took the church into every corner of the Roman Empire. Sole dependence on a formally trained ministry would not, as Kenneth Latourette points out,[1] have enabled the early church to expand so rapidly.

In Alexandria, about 230 A.D., Origen upgraded into an advanced theological school what Clement had started as an informal adult Bible study. The subjects included Bible training, natural sciences, geometry, astronomy, philosophy, and ethics. The church was faced with devastating attacks from philosophic critics and consequently needed a ministry to defend the faith. Theological education in this part of the Roman Empire assumed the form of a school of religious apologetics. Its curriculum was not shaped by an arbitrary standard, but by a practical need.

This formal pattern of theological education in schools was not followed in the fourth and fifth centuries. Rather, the clergy received ministerial training, often from an early age, through personal tutorial sessions with a bishop and older priests.

By the beginning of the sixth century the structure of the Roman Empire was collapsing. Invasions by Goths, Vandals, Franks, Visigoths, and Lombards rent the fabric of classical civilization and brought culture to such a low ebb that the ensuing period is sometimes referred to as the "Dark Ages." If the light of the orthodox Christian faith and culture was to shine in Southern and Western Europe, outposts for evangelism and civilization must be established. The form adequate to perform this function, as well as to train a portion of the church's leadership, was the monastery.

Many of these monasteries were staffed by missionaries from England and Ireland. As their work of conversion and civilization progressed, they took young boys into the monastery and trained them to be monks. The curriculum was a simple one of reading, writing and memorizing much of the Bible. Included also was basic doctrine and some knowledge of the liturgy.

Today we talk about penetrating the world. At this period of church history the task was to escape from the pollution of the world and to reestablish a Christian culture into which the non-Christians could be invited. The monastery form does not fulfill the function of today's church, but without it Christianity would not have survived in Western Europe.

The episcopal school was another form of ministerial training in the medieval period. Here again was the tutorial method with a group of students gathered around a bishop to receive training in church dogma, liturgy and canon law. At an earlier time their secular education came through the ordinary Roman schools of the day. When the Roman system of classical education was destroyed by the barbarian invasions, the episcopal schools, as well as the monasteries, assumed the responsibility of giving the secular training upon which the theological education was based. These episcopal schools formed one strand of the movement which ultimately led, in the twelfth and thirteenth centuries, to the founding of Europe's first universities--institutions whose *raison d'etre* was the teaching of theology.

INFLUENCE OF THE REFORMATION

As a result of the Protestant Reformation, the Bible was rediscovered. Believers in the evangelical churches desperately wanted to understand God's Word. Consequently, a great emphasis was placed upon catechetical preaching that would explain Biblical truth. Every church had at least one daily service with a sermon, and some churches had several such services. One great need, then, was a leadership that would meet the need of the churches for Biblical instruction. Little wonder that in the academy established by Calvin in Geneva preaching was central in the curriculum. Anything else would have been dysfunctional. Form and function in ministerial training were closely linked.

In seventeenth century England there was both a highly trained ministry and an untrained one. A reformation in learning had stimulated the founding of hundreds of neighborhood grammar schools throughout England. These schools trained boys for the church of England, and religion was the core of the curriculum. The grammar schools fed into English universities in which theology, again, was the central academic interest. Subjects normally associated now with the university such as science, medicine and law were pursued in other schools.

The thorough training required by the Anglicans for the ordained ministry was also a concern shared by the Puritans. In 1644 a Parliamentary ordinance was passed that required all ministerial candidates to read Hebrew and Greek.

Why did both the Anglicans and Puritans feel that at least a portion of their clergy needed this type of training? Was it an arbitrary standard? Not at all! Both groups were confronted by intellectual attacks from Roman Catholic scholars well-versed in Hebrew and Greek.

Nevertheless, a widespread ignorance existed among most of the clergy in England during the seventeenth century. Perhaps no more than one out of six had sufficient training to be ordained or licensed as preachers. "Many knew little or no Latin and less Scripture--some could barely read the English services of the new Prayer Book."[2]

Despite this lack of formal educational background, provision was made for these men to receive instruction fitting them for ministry in the smaller, more isolated parishes. They studied the Bible and Bullinger's _Decades_, a book of sermons. Licensed preachers in their vicinity supervised their studies and made quarterly reports on their academic and practical progress. Arch deacons examined them regularly and reported the results.

An important task for the ministry during this period was to catechize the parish by families and give pastoral counseling. For this purpose manuals on counseling were prepared for private study. In addition, older ministers with experience in counseling established informal training classes in their homes to give instruction in this art. The function which the church and its ministry must perform was implemented by the form of theological education.

During this period of English history, some questioned the need for a partly or fully trained ministry. The role of the laity was emphasized, and schooling was thought unnecessary. The need for a converted ministry caused piety to be given priority over formal education. Some claimed that since the ministry is a Divine calling God alone can do the equipping. Others asked why Hebrew and Greek were necessary if the original manuscripts were not extant. And obviously God did use men without the proper education--John Bunyan being the most notable example.[3]

THEOLOGICAL EDUCATION IN AMERICA

When the Puritans settled in New England they brought their concept of the ministry with them. They expected their clergymen, who would form the intellectual elite of New England, to be well-trained men. This stress upon educational qualifications led to the founding of Harvard College in 1636, and in the ensuing colonial period nine colleges were founded which had similar purposes.

College training was intended to give the minister his basic general education. Specific theological instruction was acquired through study under the supervision of established clergymen. These clergymen, in some instances, were ministerial professors who used the college as a base from which to go out and train ministerial candidates in various areas.

In other cases, the clergymen who did the training were parish ministers who opened up their homes to students, provided them with room and board, guided their study and afforded them practical experience in ministerial duties.

During the first half of the eighteenth century, in the middle colonies, it was the custom for Presbyterian churches to have pastors trained in the universities or colleges in Ireland, Scotland or New England. Several difficulties made this pattern unacceptable to some. If the pastors originally came to the middle colonies from these other areas, it was not easy to learn much about their background. It was expensive to go abroad or to New England for study. Furthermore, there was no certainty that the students would return, and, if they did, it was only with difficulty that they could fit into the local situation.

Meanwhile, another form of ministerial training had developed. William Tennant had come to Pennsylvania as a boy of thirteen. He received most of his education from his father and concluded that if he could learn in this fashion, it would be possible for others as well. He made this vision a reality by establishing the "log cabin" school in Bucks County, Pennsylvania, where he taught and prepared local men for the ministry. The facility was not ideal--a roughly formed structure only twenty feet by twenty feet. The studies, however, included what normally was received in a university plus a training in divinity.

The Synod objected to this type of theological education. One man, they claimed, could not give a thorough education. Moreover, piety seemed to be exalted over knowledge.

Particular needs on the American frontier led to another very functional form of theological education. Here the cry was for evangelists--those experienced and gifted in leading men to personal decision for Christ. The intellectual church leaders or parish ministers of the Atlantic seaboard were not what the situation demanded.

Evangelists were produced by a type of extension training. Personal study, a circuit of preaching points, periodic tutoring, and quarterly examinations were utilized to prepare men who conquered the frontier for Christ. These Methodist and Baptist circuit riders on the frontier used stumps, blocks, old logs and wagon beds for their pulpit. Wherever they were is where the school was! One of these men, Peter Cartwright, made fun of the intellectual Easterners, but he himself had studied literary theological books under an elder and had been examined quarterly. His education was not an inferior one, but a different one. More important, his training was functional to his calling.

This pattern on the American frontier was indebted greatly to the Wesleyan movement in England. Although Wesley's circuit riders were extremely busy in their itinerant ministry their formal education was not neglected. Some of these preachers claimed that to study the Bible was enough. To this Wesley retorted, "If you need no books but the Bible, you are above St. Paul. If you have no taste for reading, then get a taste for it or return to your trade." When they objected that they had no books to study, Wesley answered, "I will give each of you as fast as you can read them books to the value of five pounds."

True to his word he published a Christian library of forty volumes for his preachers and demanded that they study five hours a day while they preached the Word of God. As a result of this procedure Wesley claimed that, "There was not one of them who could not pass an examination in substantial, practical, experimental divinity, as few of our candidates for holy orders even in the University."[4]

The Dutch Reformed Church founded the first separate theological seminary in America at Flatbush, Long Island, New York, in 1774. However, this form of theological education did not become popular until the early nineteenth century when seventeen permanent institutions were established.[5]

The decisive turning point in American theological education was the independence of the colonies. At this juncture professional schools arose in law and medicine, and it seemed natural that theological training should follow suit. With beginning disestablishment of religion in the thirteen states a new spirit of competition developed among the denominations. Each group wanted its own school to perpetuate its own distinctives. The conviction also increased among many that one man was unable to effectively train in the many, varied aspects of the ministry.

The separate seminary did not replace other forms of theological education. Methodist preachers continued to be educated on horseback. One man reports how he reviewed grammar as he rode to his engagements. He parsed sentences while he visited with friends. During one year his reading diet was twenty-five books of history and theology. His teacher was a local preacher. Another lamented that his "facilities" for study were not equal to those in fine libraries, but that "he had some acquaintance with the Hebrew and Greek languages."[6]

The separate theological training school has been the most commonly perpetuated form for the training of the ministry in younger churches around the world. Unfortunately, the impression is often given that this is the only form that God has provided for his church. Where this conviction has taken hold of mission and church leaders, great resistance has developed to different patterns that may be more functional.

NEW EXPERIMENTS

As theories of progressive education have gained currency in the West, the environment has been created for innovative approaches in both general and theological education. Moreover, new approaches to the form of the church and of the ministry have created a demand for new forms of theological education.

McCormick Theological Seminary in Chicago has adopted a program of Individualized Guided Education, the first step of which is to complete a basic level of studies. Each student will follow this level at a speed commensurate with his own background, ability, and maturity. Resources available to him are personal counseling by his faculty advisor, a syllabus of courses, projects, seminars, specimens of the qualifying examinations and a clear statement of the faculty expectations for student achievement. No student will follow exactly the same route in reaching this initial goal.

After completing his qualifying examinations, the student is aided in structuring an individualized program of studies at a more advanced level. Here again his work is personalized in terms of his achievement, his interests and his needs in present and future ministry. The content of the curriculum and the form of his study program are highly functional.[7]

Many seminaries are developing their programs in close relationship with action training centers. Two insights have guided these efforts: Theology can only by understood in life situations as a "doing theology." Students have too frequently been "recruited from the religious ghetto, trained in an insulated seminary and returned to the sheltering religiosity of the status quo church."[8]

Saint Paul School of Theology in Kansas City has been an innovator in this emphasis of "action and reflection." In the student's first year he is required to be involved each of three quarters in a minimum of six hours weekly in a specific mission in the world. During the summer of 1970, seven conservative evangelical seminaries cooperated in the Urban Ministry Program for Seminarians (UMPS) in Chicago's inner city. At least four hours of academic credit were given to each student participant by his respective institution.

Episcopalians have been involved in a unique experiment in theological education in Los Angeles. Students are men with successful careers in law, medicine, business and education who are seriously considering the possibility of the ministry. They need not leave their vocations or their families to go away to school. Classes are held on Friday evenings and Saturday. The curriculum is the same as that of the regular five-day seminary program. At the end of four years a basic decision must be made. If the student opts for a ministry in the church, he leaves his job, studies in a resident institution for one year, and then actively enters a church vocation. If, after these four years of study and evaluation, he feels that he is not gifted for a full-time church ministry, he continues in his secular vocation and serves Christ as a committed and knowledgeable layman.

Fuller Theological Seminary has established an extension center to offer credit in degree work in Fresno, California. In this center, operated in cooperation with the Mennonite Brethren Biblical Seminary, the professor is in contact with his students a maximum of three or four times in a ten-week quarter. Guided study, research papers, periodic seminars, and a final examination are being utilized in these non-resident courses.[9]

Innovations of this type in theological training are paralleled in the field of general education. One of the most interesting of these is the open university in Great Britain. This school, which commenced offering courses in January, 1971, will provide educational opportunity leading to a university degree for older men and women who can neither forsake jobs or families in order to be internal students for several years on the campus. In describing this innovative educational program, one writer observes that it will "tap the great unused reservoir of human talent and potential."[10] This is the goal of the extension theological seminary--to tap God-equipped men with ability to pastor existing churches and to plant new ones. Missionaries and national church leaders will be more open to this possibility as they see the variety of forms that God has given his church throughout history for ministerial training.

NOTES FOR CHAPTER 6

1. Kenneth Latourette, A History of the Expansion of Christianity, Vol. 1, The First Five Centuries, New York, Harper, 1937, p. 116.

2. Richard Niebuhr and Daniel Williams (ed.), The Ministry in Historical Perspective, New York, Harper, 1956, p. 186.

3. Ibid., p. 206.

4. C. W. Ransom, The Christian Minister in India, London, Lutterworth Press, p. 267.

5. Niebuhr and Williams, The Ministry, Ch. 8.

    Also see Robert Kelly, Theological Education in America, New York, George H. Doran Company, 1924, p. 25.

6. Frederick Norwood, "Americanization of the Wesleyan Itinerant," in Gerald McCullah (ed.), The Ministry in the Methodist Heritage, Nashville, Board of Education of the Methodist Church, 1960, p. 55.

7. Arthur McKay, "McCormick Theological Seminary," *Nexus*, Vol. 12, Spring, 1969, pp. 27-30.

8. W. Paul James, "Action Training and the Seminaries: Four Possibilities," *Theological Education*, Winter, 1970, pp. 152-159.

9. *Theology News and Notes*, Fuller Theological Seminary, November, 1970, p. 14.

10. "The Open University," *Expository Times*, April, 1970, 81:7, p. 224.

7

"TRAINING IN THE STREETS" IN CHILE

We have seen that throughout the history of the Christian church many different forms of theological training have been used to advantage for the development of the ministry. Even today some churches outside of the main stream so well known in the traditionally Protestant countries have developed forms of ministerial training quite unlike anything we have been used to. One of the most unusual, and at the same time successful, forms has been developed through the years in the indigenous Pentecostal churches of Chile. In order to understand it, let's take an imaginary visit to that long, thin country on South America's west coast.

We plan our visit so that we are in the capital city of Santiago on a Sunday. Around five o'clock we take a bus and get off anywhere around the railroad station, then begin walking down one of the larger streets. If we look both ways at every intersection, it will not be long before we spot a crowd on a street corner or in a small plaza. Immediately we hear either singing or a voice coming over the portable amplifier, and we know we have found one of the several open air meetings held by groups from the Methodist Pentecostal Church, one of the larger indigenous groups in Chile.

As we approach the crowd, which might number between fifty and 300, we make sure we have our Bibles in our hands in plain sight. With these we will be accepted as *hermanos*, and no one will try to convert us on the spot. Our group might include 75 other people with Bibles under their arms. Maybe fifteen or twenty will have guitars and accordions, long red sashes flowing from the guitars. Between songs, three or four will step up to the microphone and give their personal testimony of how God saved them from drink, adultery, wife-beating, stealing, and cheating, and gave them a new life. They will recommend the same to the group of curious onlookers gathered around. "Glorias" and "amens" will ring out from the other Christians from time to time.

When the meeting is finished, the listeners are not asked to come to church "sometime" and given a tract. They are invited to "come along" with the crowd to church that very night. Many decide to go, the group begins to march through the street singing and reciting Bible verses in unison, and then stops for a similar meeting on another street corner.

The leader keeps check on his watch, and at the proper time the final parade begins toward what is known as the Jotabeche Church, bringing the newly-found visitors along with them. The same thing had been happening in virtually every neighborhood within parading distance of the church. At about seven o'clock the several groups converge on the church from all sides. No motor traffic moves on Jotabeche Street at this time. The church officers come out in front of the church and form two lines of welcome, while the open-air campaigners file between them and enter the church building, singing the praises of Zion.

The several Chilean Pentecostal denominations (most of which are splits from one another and have a common ancestry) trace their beginnings to a Pentecostal revival in the Methodist Church in 1909, and a break from Methodism by Rev. Willis Hoover. Other than Hoover, these churches, which comprise over 80 percent of Chilean Protestantism now, have had no missionary influence of any consequence. Unlike many other churches in Latin America they have been free to develop along cultural lines which are indigenous to the Chileans, and therefore many things they do seem strange to other Protestants, both Latin Americans and Anglo-Saxons. But they do not seem strange to Chileans, and a result has been one of the fastest-growing churches in Latin America.

The half hour between seven and seven thirty, for example is a bedlam of noise and confusion. Singing stops, but a social time begins. Everyone greets everyone else, asks about their family's health, tells what the Lord has done for them during the past week, and shares in a time of fellowship. Anyone who wants a good seat has to get there early. The Jotabeche Church (at least the last time I went) seats only 5,000, and the overflow has to listen through loudspeakers in the street. The orchestra, composed mostly of guitars and accordions, gathers in the balcony--500 strong--and tunes the instruments, forming a background of musical cacophony to the chattering below.

A few minutes after seven thirty, pastor Javier Vasquez steps on the platform with the ten or so others who will take part in the service. The noise stops, and the service begins. Faces radiate joy--the people would rather be in church than anywhere else in the world. During the special numbers or hymns a dozen or two will stand and begin to dance through the aisles in rhythm to the music with upraised hands. Some prayer times will sound like a free-for-all, but they will all stop at a signal, keeping everything decent and in order. Instead of passing offering plates, the pastor invites all 5,000 to come up front and leave their offerings at the altar, causing a seeming mass confusion, but a pattern well accepted by the congregation. After the service a long line forms in front of the pulpit to shake hands with the pastor, give him a present, or have him pray briefly for their health or some spiritual problem.

Although I haven't been able to double check this, I was told in Santiago that when Javier Vasquez was elected pastor of the church, he received 40,000 secret ballot votes! These came not only from the Jotabeche Church itself, since that is only the "mother church." Some 35 daughter churches also participated in the election. Little wonder that most Chilean politicians are interested in keeping on the good side of the evangelicals there!

Vasquez has his church organized like an army. Not only do the open air teams go out on Sunday afternoon, but an elite corps of around eighty bicycle riders in red and white uniforms go out with guitars and Bibles to many parts of the city outside of walking distance. One Tuesday night Pastor Vasquez invited me to speak to his men's group. A fierce wind and rainstorm drenched the city about an hour before the meeting, and lasted through the night. I thought the meeting might be called off, but went along with wet shoes and all. Vasquez apologized to me that only 400 men had come that night! I learned that they form what is called the "volunteer army," several hundred men who put themselves at the orders of the pastor to move out in any type of ministry--hospital or jail visitation, praying for the sick, open air meetings, planting of new churches--or what have you. They are all working men who support their families well with their jobs, but give their spare time to the work of the Lord.

One of the phenomena of the Chilean Pentecostals is what has been called "growth by splits." A man like Pastor Vasquez obviously has outstanding gifts of leadership. He knows how to manage his huge church with the skill of an army general. He has many characteristics of the type of man called a *caudillo* in the political world in Latin America. Most of the growing Pentecostal churches in Chile are led by pastors of the *caudillo* type, which is a familiar and well-accepted pattern among the Chileans. But the disadvantage is that there is seldom room for two *caudillos* in the same church. As Catholic sociologist Emilio Willems says: "Two opposing principles are operative in the Pentecostal sects, one 'democratic' and the other 'authoritarian.' They clash as soon as rival leaders with similar divine endowments arise and accuse the ones in power of misusing their authority or, as they sometimes put it, of 'antidemocratic behavior.' If the rival is able to sway enough followers, the split occurs and a new sect is born. There is much bitterness during the conflict, and such words as 'caudillo' and 'cacique' are freely used, but little of it seems to remain once the secession has taken place."[1] Back in 1942, for example, Bishop Enrique Chavez had come up through the ranks in the Jotabeche Church, but he found no room at the top. In *caudillo* style he split off from the Methodist Pentecostals in 1946, took some people with him, and started his own denomination called The Pentecostal Church of Chile. According to Jesuit Ignacio Vergara, in only ten years Chavez' work was "enormous." Not only did he have a central church which was a "virtual basilica," but that mother church had given birth to 26 other congregations, and a total of 136 preaching points.[2] Statistics in Chile are hard to come by, but estimates of current membership of Bishop Chavez' church run from 13,500 (Read, Monterroso and Johnson) to over 60,000 (Chavez). According to Kessler, Chavez "does not share the horror for church division which is usually felt in ecumenical circles." He believes "that division has helped the astonishing growth of the Pentecostal churches in Chile more than it has hindered it."[3] Read, Monterroso and Johnson say, "The influence of strong personalities vying for leadership has produced a proliferation of Pentecostal groups and denominations. The dynamic force behind a newborn church creates a certain spiritual momentum that results in growth."[4]

Not only did Chavez' split-off grow, but so did the church he split from. Just this year the Jotabeche Church left the building that could hold only 5,000 and moved into a gigantic new edifice that seats 16,000, has rooms for 200 overnight guests, and boasts its own independent water and electrical supply. It was all built with Chilean money--not a cent of foreign subsidy!

HOW THE LEADERS ARE TRAINED

The question we have been leading up to is this: how are leaders like Vasquez and Chavez trained? It is hard to believe at first, but none of the great leaders of the Chilean Pentecostal churches have been for one day to a seminary or Bible institute. The training system of these churches is so different from what other churches have developed in the twentieth century, that it remained a complete mystery to most outsiders. In fact it was commonly said that the pastors were "untrained," and scores of others felt very sorry for the Chilean Pentecostal ministers.

Now the picture is clearer. A brilliant study published by sociologist Christian Lalive D'Epinay in 1967 has given the rest of the world light on the matter. Now we can understand the inner operation of this strange, but highly successful, method of "training in the streets."[5]

Using a slightly different analogy and classification, Lalive's findings can be described as seven rungs on the ladder up to the pastorate. Anyone can start, in fact all are expected to try the first rung. Any of the six rungs may break, sending the candidate back to the ranks. The rungs may be described as follows:

1. <u>Street preaching</u>. When a person is converted, he or she is expected to give his testimony in public in a street meeting the very next Sunday. Experience will show that some are gifted and successful in this ministry and if so they can go up to the next rung.

2. <u>Sunday School class</u>. Sunday School meets on Sunday morning. If the teacher can communicate simple Bible truths to his students, and hold the interest of the class, he may be advanced to a more important class, and he passes this test.

3. <u>"Preacher."</u> As a "preacher," the candidate is permitted to lead worship and is asked to bring messages on occasion. If his pastor is pleased with his performance, he will promote him to the following rung.

4. <u>New preaching point</u>. When he is sent out to a new preaching point (*avanzada*), his success is measured in an objective way--he must produce converts to demonstrate to others that God has given him the gifts necessary for the ministry. If he does, his position can become official on the next rung.

5. <u>Christian worker</u>. Upon application to the Annual Conference of pastors, he is proposed and accepted as a Christian worker (*obrero del Senor*). This gives him an official title for the first time, and he is under the orders of the denominational leadership.

6. <u>Pastor-deacon</u>. He is assigned an area (*viña nueva*) in which he is expected to plant a church. As this takes place he may be named pastor-deacon. If he does not gain converts and form the nucleus of a new church, he goes no higher, nor does he receive the title.

7. <u>Pastor</u>. The probationer (*probando*) then comes up against his last test. In order to be promoted to pastor, he must present sufficient evidence to the Annual Conference that he can leave the secular world, dedicate his full time to the ministry, and be financially supported in it by the congregation he has gathered together.

As we have seen in the preceding chapter, this is not the first time in history that the Christian church has used the apprenticeship system to train the ministry. But it is one of the least known cases today, and an example of a system that seems to work. The result is one of the fastest growing complexes of churches in Latin America.

This is no three-year Bible institute program. It may take the candidate twenty years to reach the top rung. But by the time he reaches it, both he and the church are quite certain that he has the gifts, the spirituality, and the dedication needed for the Christian ministry. One of the results of such a long process is that 57 percent of the pastors are over fifty years of age. Also 56 percent have less than six grades of primary school. But they are God's men for the job, and as such officially recognized by their churches.

Few seminary-trained pastors receive the affection and allegiance of their people that the Chilean Pentecostal pastors do. David Brackenridge describes the pastor's position in these words: "It is astonishing to note the care and reverence the people show towards their pastor. Everything is done for him. Besides monetary support, members bring gifts of meat, vegetables and fruit. His table is usually full. He entertains lavishly and no member is turned away who is in need. But it must be said that the pastor controls everything--finances and all the activities. Nothing is done without his consent."[6]

Curiously, through the years many of the relatively static, non-growing denominations have tried to help the Pentecostals improve their ministerial training. This was partly the reason why the conciliar groups set up the Theological Community in Santiago some years ago. The U.S.A. Assemblies of God also expected that the indigenous Pentecostal churches would use their Bible institute in Santiago. Others have tried; all have been notably unsuccessful. The Pentecostals prefer "training in the streets." As a matter of fact, the top leaders consistently turn down lavish scholarship offers, knowing that if they enter some institution they will lose their status in most of the churches. Lalive makes this astute commentary: "Without claiming that there may be a *causal* relationship between the theological level of the pastors and the evangelical dynamism of their denominations, the existence of correlation between these two facts makes us less confident of the benefits of theological education, and even of the method of training in the developed countries which we impose on Protestants in the developing nations."[7]

One disadvantage of training in the streets becomes evident to the observer who listens to the sermons preached by the pastors from the pulpits of these churches. This is the appalling lack of theological and even biblical content. The susceptibility of such a large mass of Christians to the entrance of some heresy is terrifying to one who holds in high esteem the "faith once delivered to the saints." God has seemed to protect the Chileans against this to now, although similar groups in Brazil and Mexico have developed a very low (not to say erroneous) doctrine of the Trinity, for example.

It seems to us who are working in extension theological education that this system could be used to great advantage to the Chilean Pentecostals. They may need it, they may not. Lalive says, "Who should be teaching whom? What right have the Presbyterians and Methodists to teach the Pentecostals, who are a living illustration of the fact that quality of faith has nothing to do with lucidity of dogmas or with perfection of discipline?"[8] This has been presented to them, but predictably the response has been much less than enthusiastic.

When I recently told a group of pastors in Viet Nam about the frustration that the indifference of the Chilean Pentecostals to extension produced, one of them raised his hand and said he had a suggestion. "This might take a longer time than you have," he said, "but I know how you could convince them. Just go there, climb up the ladder to the seventh rung, and then tell them about extension."

He was right!

NOTES FOR CHAPTER 7

1. Emilio Willems, Followers of the New Faith, Vanderbilt University Press, 1967, pp. 113-114.

2. Ignacio Vergara, El Protestantismo en Chile, Santiago, Editorial del Pacifico, 1962, p. 163.

3. J. B. A. Kessler, Jr., A Study of the Old Protestant Missions and Churches in Peru and Chile, Goes, Oostervaan & le Cointre N.V., 1967, p. 318.

4. William R. Read, Victor M. Monterroso, and Harmon A. Johnson, Latin American Church Growth, Grand Rapids, Eerdmans, 1969, p. 104.

5. Christian Lalive d'Epinay, "The Training of Pastors and Theological Education, the Case of Chile," *International Review of Missions*, Geneva, W.C.C., Vol. LVI, N . 222, April, 1967, pp. 185-192.

6. Brackenridge quoted by J. B. A. Kessler, A Study of the Older Protestant Missions . . ., p. 318.

7. Christian Lalive, "The Training of Pastors . . ." p. 185.

8. Ibid., pp. 185-186.

8

THE BIRTH OF
THE EXTENSION SEMINARY

The extension seminary was born in Latin America. Part of the web of circumstances which brought this about can now be reduced to some clear statistical data. Rough as this data might be, it still sketches the broad outlines of one of the world's most serious "ordination gaps."

The influential book, <u>Latin American Church Growth</u>, estimates the number of evangelical (Protestant) churches in Latin America at 75,000.[1] Whereas each one of these churches has leaders, it is estimated that only 15,000 of them have enjoyed what might be considered adequate theological training. This leaves 60,000 who still need training. As has been mentioned previously, these are almost invariably mature men whose leadership ability and spiritual gifts have been tried and found true.

Many think that 60,000 is a highly conservative estimate. They talk of recent statistics of Brazil alone where of some 16,000 who hold the title of "pastor" (they are functionally ordained), 11,500 of them have not had formal theological training. This would be par for the course, if it were not for some 40,000 others in Brazil who are actually leading congregations, but who do not even have the title of pastor. Many of them are termed "lay pastors." As a matter of fact, 100,000 untrained church leaders in Latin America might be the best figure, admitting that it is largely a symbolic number.

The present efforts to train these leaders are dramatically described by Read, Monterroso and Johnson: "At the present rate of growth, approximately 5,000 new congregations are formed in Latin America each year. If all the students in the 360 existing theological training institutions were to become pastors after graduation, there still would be an insufficient supply of pastors for the new congregations alone, to say nothing of those already existing."[2]

The 100,000 are doing their best. God has gifted them and they are faithfully using their gifts. But understandably, many of them feel personal frustration when they come to the self-realization that they are considered second class pastors because they have not had formal training, and that under the traditional system of theological education they find it virtually impossible to make up for their deficiency. It is not surprising that their congregations often suffer from spiritual malnutrition, and that some missionaries from well-fed congregations under skillful pastoral care in the homelands hastily judge their Latin American brethren as being terribly "unspiritual." The 100,000 would dearly like to remedy the situation, and this is one of the reasons why the new extension system has been so well received in these circles.

Perhaps the most insidious danger lurking within the complex of the Latin American ordination gap is the possibility that large segments of the Latin American church will fall away into heresy. As Ralph Winter has said: "The greatest *encouragement* in missions today is that the Christian movement is outrunning the traditional methods of ministerial training, but the greatest *tragedy*, both in the U.S. and abroad, is that we are ecclesiastically and institutionally arthritic at the point of *bending* to give appropriate, solid, theological education to the real leaders that emerge in the normal outworking of our internal church life. Without this critical retooling of our theological education, church growth may in many areas wander into Mormon-type heresies instead of producing a Biblically-based evangelicalism. In some places this is already happening before our eyes.[3]

THE GUATEMALA EXPERIMENT

Some years before these general statistical studies were made for Latin America as a whole, the Presbyterian Church in Guatemala did some mathematical work of its own. They had an excellent seminary of the traditional cut in the capital, Guatemala City, and it had been serving the denomination for twenty-five years. But in 1962 the leaders took an inventory, and discovered that in twenty-five years the seminary had prepared only ten pastors who were actively serving the denomination. This in itself was quite a startling realization, but more so was a glance into the future. At that time only five or six students were enrolled in the seminary, hardly sufficient to take care of the 200 growing churches which belonged to the Presbyterian denomination.

Such a dramatic ordination gap indicated that something was wrong somewhere. It was not atypical of other churches in Latin America, but in his providence, God had raised up a special trio of missionaries and placed them together in Guatemala at that time. The three were thoroughly evangelical in their convictions, burdened for the training of the ministry, concerned about the future growth of the Presbyterian Church in Guatemala, and unusually creative in their thinking. Ralph Winter, for example, had gone through a hodge-podge of academic disciplines that dovetailed perfectly for the situation God put him in. His university training (and family background) was engineering (Cal Tech), his masters degree in education (Columbia), his doctorate in anthropology (Cornell), and his B.D. from Princeton. James Emery was a General Electric engineer-cum-theologian and a Hartford graduate in anthropology, who had become an expert in the Indian cultures of Guatemala. Ross Kinsler, a theologian-pastor, with his doctorate from Edinburgh, joined these two innovators to complete the team of God's educational pioneers. Together the three cross-fertilized each other's ideas and set themselves to come up with some answer to their church's ordination gap.

The Guatemala trio was thoroughly familiar with the several solutions that others had previously attempted to train those who could not enter traditional seminaries. They studied the possibilities of offering more scholarship help, of changing their academic year around, of correspondence courses, of night schools, of regional laymen's training institutes, and of other methods. None of these fitted their particular set of problems.

Finally they realized that one of the major difficulties was that their seminary was located in Guatemala City, while the majority of their churches were located out in the rural areas in the western part of the country. It became evident that the leaders they wanted to train were not going to come to Guatemala City for training, so they concluded that part of the solution lay in moving the seminary out to the region where their churches were located. Because of the multiplicity of sub-cultures and different academic levels they first experimented with separate training programs for each ethnic group, but "it only produced a caste system, dividing rather than uniting the church."[4]

After much predictable debate among the Guatemalan leaders, the Church came to the radical decision of selling their seminary in the city, and using the funds to build a new campus out in the town of San Felipe, located in the midst of their most dense cluster of churches. Once the new seminary campus was

The Birth of the Extension Seminary 73

built, another major problem raised its head. The church leaders still did not matriculate in the seminary! The trouble was that the seminary in San Felipe had simply moved geographically, but it had kept its same structure.

A radical change in structure was the solution proposed. The seminary obviously was too centralized--everything was located in one place, and the church leaders could not adjust their lives to fit into a program that required extended periods of residence away from their homes. It made little difference if the residence center was in far off Guatemala City or in nearby San Felipe. Such an adjustment was simply not possible for the majority.

From this sprang the idea of the decentralized seminary. If the leaders couldn't come to the seminary, the seminary could be broken up into pieces with a piece placed within easy reach of each interested church leader. Residence in a central institution then would not be required, but the important principle was that no matter where a piece of the seminary might be located the students would be receiving the same theological training they would have received if they had gone to San Felipe to live. This was no short term laymen's institute that gave good teaching but that could not prepare men for Presbyterian ordination. It was to be first class ministerial training.

Several regional centers were thus set up, where the student would meet once a week with a professor from the seminary, receive help on his studies of the previous week, and take home assignments for the coming week. The same textbooks used in the residence program were the basis of the study program.

The new structure seemed to work. Enrollment increased at once from seven to fifty students. Finally the real church leaders were studying in the seminary. But the next major problem in the experiment soon became evident: the students were not learning much! Somehow the educational process had broken down.

The minds of the engineers went to work, using that enviable ability to erase the past and focus on the present problem and its solution. Here a graduate degree in education also helped. By 1963 the value of programmed, self-instructional study materials had been widely accepted by educational psychologists. The trio decided that if the traditional textbooks were inadequate for the new structure, they would set out to write new textbooks that were. Thus began the most physically and emotionally trying phase of the project. Gallons of midnight oil as well as grueling self-discipline were needed as this first generation of extension materials was produced, tested, and revised. Although the materials were primitive as compared to what is being done today, they seemed to work. They were written in such a way that the student took active participation in the learning process as he worked through them. Eventually tests showed that many of the extension students were pulling better grades in the same subjects as the residence students! The shape of the future was beginning to take form in Guatemala.

But even the self-instructional materials had to be prepared to teach a student who had reached a predetermined academic level. Those who were more advanced or too far behind academically did not learn as much as they should from the books. The design of the materials was varied somewhat to make them multi-level so that each student could study at his own level. In the same seminary, then, students ranging from sixth-grade graduates to university men were studying, each at his appropriate level.

Two-thirds of the church leaders who should have been studying, however, did not have the six grades of primary necessary to study at the lowest level. How to solve this problem? These men could not be by-passed. Two alternatives were possible: lower the seminary requirements or raise the level of the leaders. Both these alternatives have subsequently been used to advantage. In the George Allan Seminary in Bolivia, for example, mature men who have had only a second-grade level of studies are taking approved theological training. In the Guatemalan Presbyterian Church, however, a higher academic level of the ministry is insisted upon for ordination. The level of the church leaders had to be raised there.

In order to accomplish this, a set of materials was prepared which would allow the leaders to bring themselves up to sixth grade levels. This was not a part of the seminary program, but it was encouraged by the seminary. Books on natural sciences, geography, mathematics, hygiene, Spanish, and Bible were prepared by Guatemalan educators. Then the government was approached to see if it would grant a sixth-grade diploma to men who had studied these materials and passed the government examinations. The government was extremely receptive to the idea, not only for church leaders, but for the population across the board. This encouraged the Lincoln Schools for adult education to be established under the leadership of Raul Echeverria, a Presbyterian layman. His materials became some of Guatemala's best-selling books, and recently he was decorated by the President with the "Order of the Quetzal,"

Guatemala's highest honor! Furthermore, scores of church leaders finally earned their primary school diplomas and enrolled in the seminary.

Looking back at this pioneer experiment in the rural area of Guatemala, the critical observer now can pick out many flaws. Since then much has been learned and much has been changed. To be true to the creative genius of the trio of architects of the extension seminary, the program must never stagnate or crystalize--it must remain pliable, constantly adapting to new situations and correcting past shortcomings.

The advantages at that time, however, far outweighed the shortcomings. Ralph Winter has listed five of the advantages which were evident to the Guatemalan educators from the beginning:

1. The door was opened for leaders who desired to reach a higher level of training.

2. The leaders could receive their theological training within the context of their own sub-culture.

3. The system permitted those students who had low motivation to leave without losing face.

4. Instead of lowering academic levels, it was observed that the extension student learns better and develops better study habits in his home.

5. The project is more economical than the conventional seminary, and it saves much time for the professor.[5]

Thus a radical departure from the traditional structure of theological education was born in the tiny Central American republic of Guatemala. It spread next to other Latin American countries.

NOTES FOR CHAPTER 8

1. William R. Read, Victor M. Monterroso, and Harmon Johnson, Latin American Church Growth, Grand Rapids, Eerdmans, 1969, p. 326.

2. Ibid.

3. Ralph D. Winter, "New Winds Blowing," Church Growth Bulletin, Vols. I - V, Donald A. McGavran, ed., South Pasadena, William Carey Library, 1969, p. 242.

4. Ralph D. Winter, "This Seminary Goes to the Student," *World Vision Magazine*, July-August, 1966, p. 11.

5. Raul Winter, *El Seminario de Extension de Guatemala*, El Seminario de Extension, informe del cursillo en Cochabamba, Bolivia, del 3 al 7 de agosto, 1968, p. 10.

9
NEW PATTERNS IN BOLIVIA AND COLOMBIA

It took some time for the extension seminary in Guatemala to catch on in other places. With the exception of the California Friends in Guatemala itself, no other theological education institutions incorporated extension programs until after a key workshop-consultation was held in Armenia, Colombia, on the campus of the Christian and Missionary Alliance Bible Institute, in September of 1967. Two of the first countries to begin their own experiments were Bolivia and Colombia, both with the school year of 1969.

The structure for the development of the extension seminary developed along quite different lines in each of these countries, and therefore they provide material for a study in contrast. Since then some projects have followed the Bolivia pattern and others the Colombia pattern. Still others have developed their own, using the high degree of flexibility inherent in extension to adapt it to their own needs.

The major difference in structure between the programs of these two South American countries was between a denominational and an interdenominational emphasis. In Bolivia, after a workshop held in August, 1968, it was decided that each denomination would do well to develop its own extension program, especially those which were already operating residential institutions, since all the existing residential institutions were associated with one particular denomination. In Colombia the presence of the United Bible Seminary, an institution relatively independent of any existing denomination, provided the rallying point for a vast interdenominational project.

BOLIVIA

The most extensively developed of the Bolivian experiments has been the George Allan Theological Seminary of the Evangelical Christian Union. The E.C.U. is Bolivia's largest evangelical denomination (not counting the Seventh-day Adventists), with an estimated 14,000 membership, some 180 churches, and 110 pastors. Another 100-200 leaders of churches and congregations have not had theological training, and therefore are not officially recognized as pastors, although many of them carry a full schedule of pastoral duties. With very few exceptions in the urban areas, the E.C.U. churches do not fully support their pastors, and thus even the recognized pastors to one degree or another are self-supporting.

The traditional theological education program of the E.C.U. was operated by the two missionary societies working with the denomination, the Andes Evangelical Mission and the Evangelical Union of South America. A.E.M. missionaries ran the Emmaus Bible Institute (urban, Spanish) and the Quillacollo Bible Institute (rural, Quechua), both of Cochabamba; the Sucre Bible Institute (rural, Quechua), and occasional institutions in Pocoata and Guayaramerin. The E.U.S.A. missionaries ran the Hebron Bible Institute in the south of the country with one rural Spanish department and one rural Guarani department.

In early 1968, Peter Savage, who had studied extension seminary principles under Ralph Winter at the Fuller Seminary School of Missions, and who had served previously in the Evangelical Seminary of Lima, went to Bolivia under the Andes Evangelical Mission. Assigned by the mission to study and evaluate the total program of theological education, he wrote a memorandum entitled "Extension Seminary Program" in March, 1968. In it he pointed out six areas in which an extension seminary program, added to the residential program already in operation, might advance the total ministerial training for the E.C.U. They included the need for simultaneous training on several different educational levels, teaching more specifically adapted to each subcultural unit, the need for continuing education for pastors of churches experiencing upward social mobility, varying cultural norms for the recognition of maturity and leadership, the problem of semiliterate church leaders incapable of abstract thought, and the danger of professionalism in the ministry.

Savage's study and subsequent leadership carried both missions and the Evangelical Christian Union into a radical restructuring of their total programs. In the First Annual

Theological Education Assembly of the E.C.U. held in August, 1968, two far-reaching changes were introduced.

The first was the creation of the George Allan Theological Seminary brought about by combining the former Emmaus and Quillacollo Bible Institutes, making them the urban and rural departments of the Seminary respectively, and adding an extension department. Savage was named by the E.C.U. as rector of the new Seminary.

The second change was to create a Theological Education Commission of the E.C.U. which would coordinate all phases of ministerial training. This, in effect, would remove the direct administration of the institutions from the foreign missions and place them under the control of the national church. With the official consent of the missions, this was established, and Savage was appointed the first Coordinator of the Commission by the E.C.U.

When the George Allan Seminary opened its doors in 1969, the extension department was ready for action, with centers in the area around Cochabamba, and on the Altiplano in Oruro and Carangas. Some of the centers succeeded, some failed. But the number of those who were studying for the ministry rose from the 65 residential students in the two Bible institutes in 1968 to 65 residential plus sixty extension students, making a total of 125 in 1969.

The program expanded in 1970 with the addition of other departments and centers. The residence enrollment fell off to fifty, but extension increased to over 150, giving a total of more than 200 students.

The George Allan Seminary now has one Rector, assisted by two Vice-Rectors, George Hilgeman for the urban (Spanish) program and Raymond Morris for the rural (Quechua and Aymara) program. Eight separate departments are led by their respective deans, including two residence departments and six extension departments. Each extension department operates a number of centers ranging at the present time from one to three, with a total of thirteen centers. This can be diagrammed as follows:

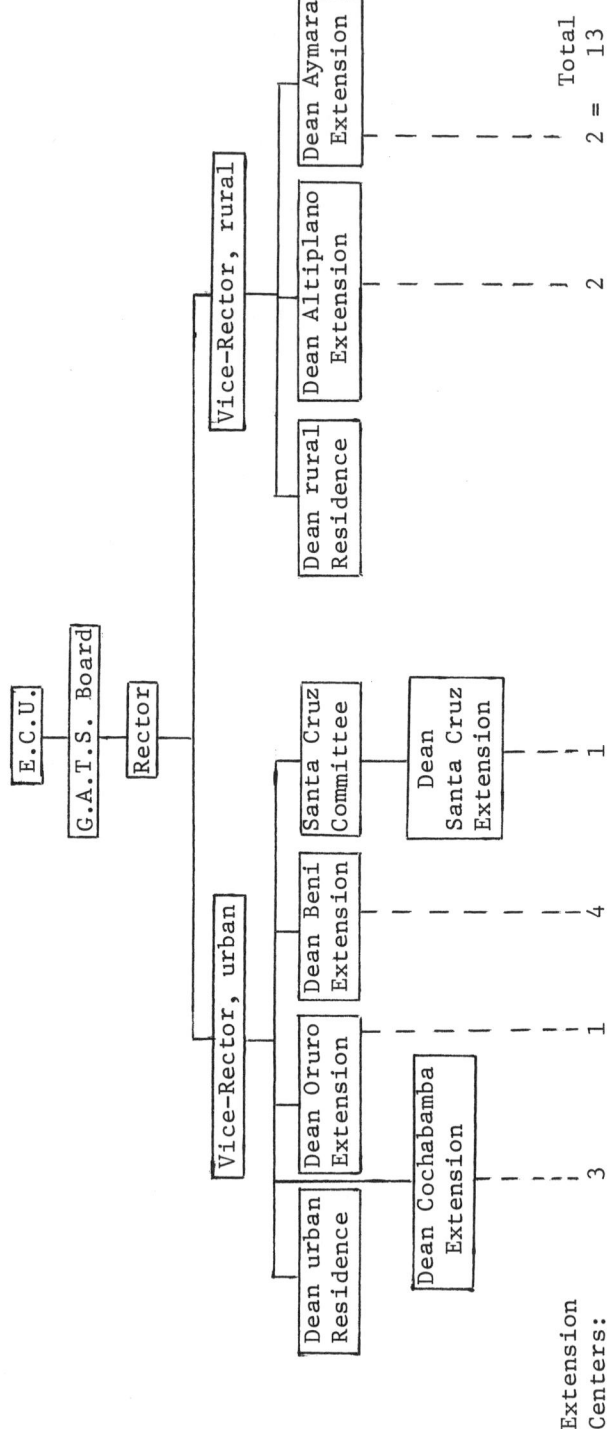

New Patterns in Bolivia and Colombia

The outstanding variation of the ordinary structure in the seminary is the Santa Cruz Extension Department. The E.C.U. has no churches in the fast-growing city of Santa Cruz, but has plans of planting churches there in the near future. The E.U.S.A. maintains resident missionaries there for itinerant work among the migrant workers. Two other faith missions, the United World Mission and the South America Mission, have churches in Santa Cruz, but no seminary or Bible institute. On their invitation, the George Allan Seminary opened an extension department in 1970, but under the administration of a local committee composed of the groups which cooperate in the department. The committee names its own dean, who also sits on the executive board of the Seminary. This gives an interdenominational flavor to at least part of the chiefly denominational seminary.

The meaning of the word "seminary" as currently being defined in Latin America should be clearly understood at this point. The decision to move from "Bible institutes" to "seminary" in the Evangelical Christian Union was not a light conclusion, but one based on a certain philosophy of theological education. More and more commonly in Latin America the word "seminary" is being defined as having an *ecclesiastical* rather than an *academic* connotation. In other words, a seminary is the place where a given church trains its ministry, no matter what the academic level or levels of that ministry might be. The academic definition, popular in the U.S.A., which assigns to a Bible institute post-high school and to a seminary post-university levels, thereby establishing two distinct academic castes is being questioned by leaders in Latin American theological education as somewhat unrealistic in their context. In the George Allan Seminary, for example, some of the students are taking theological studies on a post-second grade level, while others are working on a post-high school level. Although they use different materials, sit under different professors, and study in different class sessions, they all are students in the same seminary because they are all being trained for the ministry in the same denomination, and will be equally recognized as pastors. More detail about the academic levels will be given in the next chapter.

COLOMBIA

Since 1945 the United Bible Seminary was operated in Medellin, Colombia, under the auspices of the Oriental Missionary Society, known in Latin America as the Interamerican Mission. Although it was called "united," and the purpose of the O.M.S. was always to serve as an interdenominational seminary, while it was a conventional residence program it never became truly united. Only since its extension ministry was launched in 1968 has it been able to draw in several other churches and fulfill its original purpose.

The Andes ranges run north and south in Colombia, and the three chief cities are stacked up in the same direction. Medellin is the one to the north; Bogota, the capital, in the center; and Cali to the south. All three are important, because now the U.B.S. has departments in each of these three major cities.

In 1967 when the Armenia workshop was held in Colombia, the Christian and Missionary Alliance had become dissatisfied with its theological training program, and was going to try moving the Bible institute from Armenia to Cali. The Gospel Missionary Union had closed its institute down, and was looking to the Lord for something more satisfactory. The Armenia workshop drew them and several others together to make coordinated plans for combined residence and extension programs all over the country. The Union Bible Seminary had already opened its structures for new cooperating bodies, so it was a natural to coordinate the program.

Under the skillful leadership of Burt Biddulph, Rector of the Seminary, a major reorganization took place. The Mennonite Brethren for one thing decided to close their residence program in Cali and move into extension exclusively for the training of their ministry. Along with the C. & M.A. and the G.M.U., they began talks with the Seminary for the setting up of a Cali Division. A grass roots workshop involving pastors and teachers was held, and the Division organized. A Vice-Rector, Vernon Reimer, was named to head up the Cali Division, to be run entirely on the extension principle. Twenty-one rural extension centers were operating out of Cali according to the latest information received.

To meet the demand for theological training in Bogota, another Extension Division was set up, and Rector Burt Biddulph moved to the capital from Medellin. He organized three urban extension centers under his Division.

In Medellin the U.B.S. residence program was continued, and supplemented by one extension center. A Vice-Rector, Wayne Weld, has been placed in charge of the Medellin Division.

Through application of extension theological education principles ministerial training in Colombia has taken a new lease on life. The U.B.S. has not only extended geographically and in numbers (enrollment soared from nineteen to 156 in just one year), but it now is truly a united, interdenominational effort with participation of Christian and Missionary Alliance, the Covenant Church, General Conference Mennonites, Mennonite Brethren, Latin American Mission, and Overseas Crusades. The Gospel Missionary Union and the Weslyan Mission are loosely affiliated, but not full participants.

In other parts of Latin America, notably Brazil, where an entire organization has been set up under the leadership of Richard Sturz to coordinate extension theological education in that vast country, other projects similar to those described in Bolivia and Colombia are getting under way. According to the best estimates those involved in extension seminaries can make, the following represents the surprising growth of this movement in Latin America from its beginning in 1962 to the present:

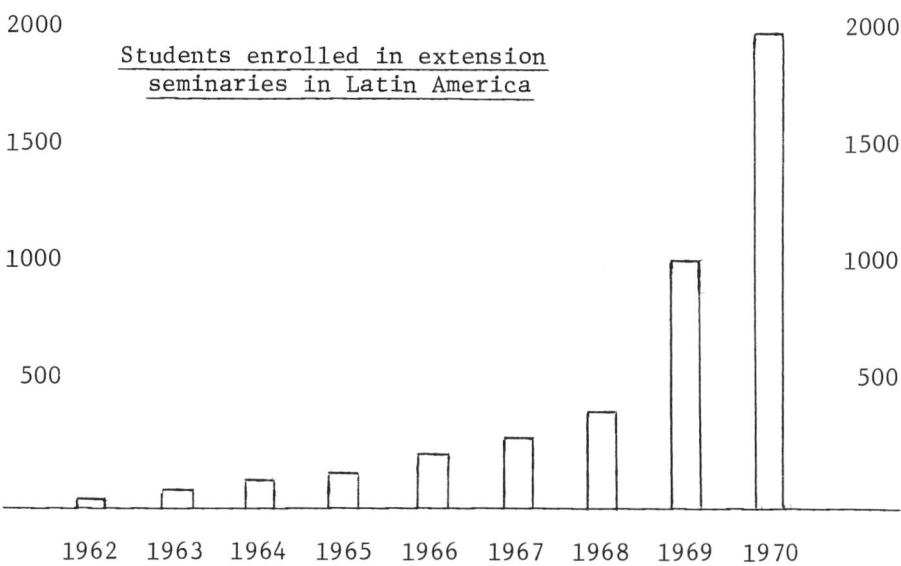

Students enrolled in extension seminaries in Latin America

10
HOW THE EXTENSION CENTER WORKS

We can no longer postpone describing some of the more practical aspects of the extension seminary. What actually happens in an extension program in full operation?

In order to understand this, we first must agree on some definitions, especially those of the different academic levels. It has already been mentioned that in many of the institutions using the extension method, students are taking their work on several different academic levels. This multi-level situation was one of the problems which seminaries and Bible institutes faced for many years in Latin America and in other places where the ministry for the younger churches was being trained. Most teachers had experienced time and time again the impossible situation of having right in the same classroom some students with a high school diploma and others with barely five or six years of primary school. To attempt to gear subject matter to reach a happy medium in such circumstances is a formidable challenge even to the most expert pedagogue.

The built-in flexibility of the extension seminary allows students on many different levels to study for the ministry, but it takes them out of the same classroom and gives them material especially designed for their particular level. Chapter 13 will describe how this material is produced, but at this point we only need to know that to operate an extension seminary properly, programmed material for each course on each level is essential.

The delegates to the Armenia workshop brought with them a large amount of cumulative experience in training pastors for the Latin American churches. As they pondered together the necessity of defining the levels at which men and women were studying in the seminaries and Bible institutes of the continent, they established a scheme of academic levels which has been accepted by nearly every institution developing extension programs. The broad outlines of the academic divisions are as follows:

Name of level	Academic prerequisites for beginning the course
Licentiate (B.D.)	Two or three years of university
Bachelor	High School diploma
Diploma	Primary School diploma (six years)
Certificate A	Two or three years of primary school
Certificate B	Little or no formal training, but functional literacy in vernacular

When students enroll in the seminary they are placed in their proper level. Many institutions have found that since they are dealing largely with mature men in the student body, their formal attainments often do not reflect their ability to handle the theological studies on a given level. Placement tests have been devised which fit each student into his proper level. This leaves room for the self-educated man to take more advanced studies, and also weeds out the person who may have slid through to a diploma on the basis of a fast tongue and winsome personality instead of actual academic attainment.

In order to describe the operation of the extension seminary, let us set up a hypothetical example, and call it Bible Theological Seminary (B.T.S.). The B.T.S. has a base institution, two extension departments, and six extension centers. One hundred twenty students are in training, forty in residence and eighty in extension.

The base institution seems to be a necessary beginning for an extension program. Whether one can operate without it remains to be seen--I have not heard of one. The base institution is usually located in a city, and is the seminary or Bible institute that is being "extended." It is the stable and visible center of activities, the institution that grants the diplomas or degrees. But it must not gain the image that it is *the* location of the seminary--wherever an extension center exists, the seminary is there also. This is an important feature of the extension mystique.

The main offices of the seminary are located in the base institution. The rector or director lives here, as does the other administrative personnel. A residence program operates here, and so perhaps a good number of the full-time faculty members are also in residence. The main library is housed on the premises. Especially for those institutions teaching on the higher levels, a first class library is obviously essential, and cannot be duplicated in every extension center. It is well to develop a general catalog of all books of the whole institution, whether the main library or the functional libraries in the centers, in the base institution.

If some of the professors of the B.T.S. are programming materials for their students, a publications department for the institution might also be located in the base institution. This may not be much more than a typewriter, a mimeograph machine, and a mailing desk, but it can be a most important element not only for the B.T.S., but also for sister institutions offering instruction in the same languages.

The forty residence students in our hypothetical seminary are all studying on the diploma and bachelor levels. But there is an extension center located here as well. This is set up for students from the city who for one reason or another cannot enroll in the residence program, but who are taking one or two extension courses. A wider variety of courses can be offered here because of the larger number of available professors. It has been found that potential faculty increases greatly when the professor only has to meet his students once a week. Some administrators, for example, who could not allow themselves to be tied down to an ordinary teaching schedule, accept an extension course because of the flexibility of the time table. First of all, the professor can arrange any time at all during the week that is mutually convenient for himself and his students. I once had a small extension class on Protestant Christianity meet in my own office, where I installed a blackboard, on Tuesdays at 1:00 - 2:00 p.m., around a pot of coffee and dessert which my wife prepared. It was a delightful learning situation!

The second advantage, time-wise, for a part-time teacher is that the preparation can be handled at more leisure. The professor does not have to prepare lectures as such. He needs to be familiar with his subject matter, of course, but does not need to develop the tightly-knit pedagogical structure of a lecture. This has already been done for him by the author of the programmed text the students are using, as will be explained in more detail in Chapter 12. His work is more in the areas of testing, counseling, and trouble-shooting. He might need as many hours per week as he would if he were lecturing, but the number of weekly deadlines is greatly reduced.

How the Extension Center Works 87

Let's say that B.T.S. extension center in the base institution holds its weekly meetings on Thursday night and at different times during Saturday. There are fifteen bachelor students and ten diploma students. On Thursday night one of the full-time professors holds an extension class in his regular seminary classroom with five of the bachelor students. Two other part-time professors, who do not teach in residence, teach extension on Saturdays, right in the seminary building. Saturday may not be the best time to teach, but for many students it is the only time they could meet with their professors, and those who have developed an extension mentality combined with their love for theological training realize that they must adjust to it.

We have said that B.T.S. has two extension departments. If we call them the Northern Department and the Southern Department we can easily distinguish them. The Northern Department is a distance from the seminary, and is self-contained. That is, no faculty members travel out from the base institution to teach there. Their faculty members are all residents in the region of the department. The dean of the department lives in Center No. 2, and he travels out to Center No. 3. The pastor of the church in Center No. 2 is also a professor, and he travels with the dean. Center No. 2 is an urban center, and the classes are held in the dean's house, some on Wednesday night and some on Saturday morning. Three are studying on the bachelor level and eight on the diploma level.

In order to identify this as an extension center, a sign painted with the same kind of lettering and the same colors as the sign over the base institution is placed over the door. This is simply a reminder that when the students enter the building usually thought of as the dean's house, they are entering the Bible Theological Seminary just as literally as they would be if they had traveled to the base institution. On Wednesday nights and Saturday mornings, that *is* the seminary. This must be stressed because it has been one of the most difficult mental adjustments for those not thoroughly familiar with extension theological education.

Center No. 3, also under the Northern Department, is located in a rural area 35 miles away. For the extension classes there, the dean and the professor get on a bus Monday afternoon, have supper with the pastor of the church there, and hold classes that night in the local church building, using the Sunday School rooms. A sign "Bible Theological Seminary" has been nailed over the side entrance to the church, making this another part of the general institution. This is the only time classes are held, so the two diploma students and twenty certificate A students all gather there. Some have to travel most of the day from their own churches to make the weekly meeting. The local pastor has built a shed-like room on the side of his house where many of these pastors from out of town sleep before traveling back the following day. The dean and the professor from Center No. 2 also stay overnight at the pastor's house.

Now is the time to pause and describe a hypothetical schedule for Center No. 3. The meeting begins at 6:30 p.m. with all 22 students present. The first half hour is a devotional time. At 7:00 the dean takes the two diploma students in the study of Romans and Galatians while the professor takes the twenty certificate students in Life of Christ. At 8:00 ten of the certificate students leave, because they have chosen to take only one course this semester. The other ten stay, and they are divided into two separate classes, the dean taking the five who have elected homiletics, and the pastor of the local church taking the five who have elected Genesis-Exodus. The professor in the meantime teaches theology to the two diploma-level students.

Each class session has several objectives. First the professor uses about ten minutes to give an examination on the materials the students had been studying the previous week. Twenty minutes is used for a discussion of the answers to the test, providing the students immediate feedback, 25 minutes for a general discussion and application of the previous week's work with the students raising any problems they might have run into, and the final five minutes going over the assignment for the following week.

At 9:00 the pastor's wife invites students and faculty alike to a cup of tea. Some have to leave early, but others sleep right there. At times lively discussions of the matters brought to the surface in the classes go on until midnight or more—an unparalleled opportunity for professors to get to know their students. The next day the dean and the professor take the bus home.

The Southern Department also has a resident dean, but no resident professors. It is near enough to the base institution so that a professor from there can assist him in two of his three centers. On Tuesday morning the professor from the base institution drives his car to Center No. 4, where the dean has traveled on the bus. The center there is a rented room in a block of stores in the business section of town. On one side is a small grocery store, on the other a barber shop. But over the room is the ubiquitous sign, "Bible Theological Seminary."

Classes are held in late morning and early afternoon for the five diploma students. Then the dean gets into the professor's car and they drive to Center No. 5.

Here, as in Center No. 3, the church becomes the seminary building on Tuesday nights, and an appropriate sign indicates it. A full night's program includes two bachelor students, three diploma students, and two certificate students. After staying at the center overnight, the professor drops off the dean at his house, and continues back to the base institution.

On Thursday the dean travels alone to Center No. 6 where he has ten certificate students in a rural community. The sign here is found nailed over the door of a thatched-roof hut which is the home of one of the students. The dean stays here also. He meets with his students for several hours during Friday, stays a second night, and travels home on Saturday.

This dean is relatively busy. He is involved every day, Tuesday through Saturday, in extension work. He does not work only eight hours a day, for in a sense he is on the job from the time he leaves his home until he arrives back. His teaching does not start and stop with the classroom. He is with his students for long periods of time. He eats meals with them, stays in their homes, meets their families, travels with them, and often stays a longer time for an evangelistic campaign or Bible teaching in their churches.

But he is only a hypothetical dean. As an example from real life, I could choose Peter Savage, Rector of the George Allan Seminary in Bolivia, where I also teach. Since most of my work is administrative, my involvement in extension is minimal--one course on the bachelor level. But Savage has involved himself more than the average.

On Thursday he boards the mission plane at 7:00 a.m., for the hour's flight to the Choro center on the bleak Altiplano. There he meets with 35 certificate students (one of whom has traveled two hours on his bicycle including crossing a shallow lake with the bicycle on his back and breaking ice with his bare feet!) until noon. He flies back to Cochabamba, takes his wife out for a game of tennis, catches up on administrative work Thursday night, begins his Friday schedule with a Greek class at 6:00 a.m. (to accommodate university students who have to be at their other classes at 8:00), meets with several classes in the Cochabamba urban extension department on Saturday, and then flies on Sunday morning to the tropical area of Bolivia where he takes the San Antonio center on Sunday, the Desengano center on Monday, the Santa Ana center on Tuesday, and flies back to Cochabamba early Wednesday morning. Charitably, the circuit which takes him to the tropical area repeats every two weeks instead of every week.

THE TEN REQUIREMENTS FOR AN EXTENSION CENTER

In order to inaugurate an extension center, ten prerequisites are necessary. I will attempt to list them here in order of priority:

1. <u>Students</u>. It is worth repeating that the extension seminary begins with the students. Here is the starting point. Never attempt to set up an extension center, and then hope that students might come. The center is where the students already are. In a year or two it might be in a different place, if the student demand shifts. For this reason, the roots of a center never should be in too deep.

2. <u>Faculty</u>. Obviously teachers are needed. Since extension makes demands upon professors that are quite different from the conventional teaching job, all teachers are not prepared to participate in extension, but the search for those who are is worth the effort.

3. <u>Self-teaching materials</u>. Either these materials must be previously available or the professors must prepare their own as they go along. More about this in Chapter 13.

4. <u>Transportation for professors</u>. Geographical problems present themselves in every extension project. Some arrangement must be made to get the professors to their centers every week. This is often the most expensive aspect of extension theological education. In some cases, such as Kalimantan in Indonesia, extension would be unthinkable without the use of aircraft.

5. <u>Classrooms</u>. A place is needed to hang the "sign," and give tangible expression to the presence of a seminary. Already several possibilities of how such a room or rooms can be provided have been mentioned. At times a rental item will have to be built into the budget.

6. <u>Furniture</u>. One of the initial capital expenditures for setting up an extension center is the purchase of a blackboard, tables, chairs, bookcases, etc. Including the cost of the functional library, a sum of $300.00 has been calculated as an average budget for establishing a center.

7. _Schedule_. The students and the professor have to agree mutually upon a schedule. A great deal of flexibility is available at this point, of course.

8. _Placement examination_. Each culture or ethnic group will need its own placement exam to see that the students are using the self-instructional material which will best be able to teach them.

9. _Functional library_. Students at the diploma level or above need a library of a limited number of books such as commentaries, Bible dictionaries, concordances, and other research material. These books are on loan from the base institution's library, and are recalled if they are not used. This is why it is called a "functional" library.

10. _Secretary_. Some person needs to be in charge of taking attendance, collecting fees, keeping the other records, and whatever else might be involved in the administration of a center. Sometimes the local pastor can do this, sometimes one of the advanced students, sometimes the dean's wife or a professor's wife. Ideally, the secretary is a person who lives at the center, not one who comes and goes.

11
OLD SHORTCOMINGS AND NEW EXPERIMENTS

The enthusiasm for extension methods which shows through on the part of its advocates should not leave the impression that this new system has no problems of its own. The extension seminary is not a panacea for all ills. Those involved in extension still have much to learn, and they intend to keep their minds open for suggestions for future improvement and innovations. In God's providence, extension may have come as a system needed for the present moment and in certain places, but perhaps just over the horizon he has still a newer form for a newer day.

The extension seminary is still a youngster. With the exception of Guatemala, most institutions using it are in their first or second years. But even in this short time, many have begun raising questions concerning the different aspects of the philosophy of extension. Some of them can be answered, some not as yet. Some simply put their finger on inherent shortcomings of the system. Here are some samples of the current dialogue:

Does the extension seminary really work? It is best not to try to answer this key question at the present time. Until a study can be made on a cross-section of *graduates* from extension institutions and compared to graduates from residential programs, any answer would be little more than a hunch. In seven years of extension the Presbyterian Seminary of Guatemala has now had about twenty graduates. Perhaps they are ready to make the first study.

Does the extension center type of meeting provide sufficient opportunity for optimum personal interaction between students and professors? Admittedly the teacher-disciple relationship with the professor in residence with his students and in close personal contact with them day after day cannot be maintained in the extension seminary. On the other hand, as we all know, a residence program does not necessarily solve the problems since many busy residence instructors have become so impersonal that they only see their students from behind a lecture desk and know their students' names as entries in a roll book.

To help solve this problem, an interesting experiment is taking place in Singapore at the present time. As an attempt to improve on the conventional residence programs, it has taken almost the opposite tack to the extension seminary. It could be termed "theological education by contraction." Using Jesus' own method as a model, they are intentionally limiting enrollment to create the lowest possible teacher-student ratio and encouraging the teachers to live with the students in a monastic type relationship. This undoubtedly will prove to be a great benefit to the students who matriculate. But the high expense and low efficiency of the system would not make much of a dent in what we have described as the "ordination gap" in Latin America, for example.

As extension programs develop, undoubtedly some extension professors will begin to gain a reputation of excellence in this new field. As they do so, one of their qualities might well be their ability to overcome the danger of too little contact with students, and find ways and means to develop a maximum of personal as well as academic influence on their students.

<u>Is not flexibility in the presentation of subject matter reduced by the use of programmed texts?</u> Yes, it is. In some cases this may be good, especially when the professor is less competent in the subject than the author of the text. But on the other hand, that daily classroom contact with the students in the residence system allows for the unexpected, existential moment when a problem emerges in class, and provides the springboard for a flash of new insight and communication. Sometimes, as all teachers know, more is accomplished during those brief moments than throughout many lecture periods. The reduction of this possibility is one of the shortcomings of the extension method, although it is not impossible that the same dynamic could occur during the weekly meetings.

<u>The rate of study is usually lengthened in extension, where the time to finish a seminary course is stretched to five, ten, or even more years. Is this not a disadvantage to the student?</u> It is true that extension is a slower process than residence. If a person can afford the time to study five subjects at once, the chances are he can afford the time to

matriculate in a residence institution, and finish in the usual three years. But since most extension education is in-service training, that is, the training of people already in the ministry of one kind or another, many students are not in a great hurry to finish. It is not as if they were anxious to finish a course in flying so they could get a job with a commercial airline and begin their careers.

On the positive side, there is a certain benefit to continuing education in any field. Pressure is being placed on all professionals to continue their education so they won't be left behind in today's rapidly-moving world. The stretched-out extension program can be considered as a kind of continuing education for the ministry, and as such an advantage of sorts.

Can programmed materials really do the job of teaching the more subjective courses and more advanced studies? Educational psychology has not given a final answer to this question as far as I know. If the delicate nuances of theology, for example, cannot be adequately taught by self-instructional materials, it will be a distinct disadvantage to extension. Of course, it must be recognized that by building in a weekly seminar between students and instructors, extension has not put all its eggs in the programmed instruction basket.

At this point we should pause to regain our perspective. We must keep in mind that for many church leaders, no option exists between residence or extension; between programmed or conventional materials. As Ross Kinsler of Guatemala has put it, "Let's be quite clear about one thing. Not one in ten of these people who make up our extension family could ever study in a traditional residence seminary, even with full scholarships. And if they could, they wouldn't be able to take the same courses in the same classrooms. And if they were by some stretch of the imagination to be trained in a residence seminary for three years, it is doubtful that they would be able to return in large numbers to their communities and churches to take up their old leadership positions either on the basis of self-support or as professional ministers."[1]

How can you provide research library facilities in the extension centers? You can't. Small, functional libraries can be provided in the extension centers, but especially on the higher levels of training where the students are expected to engage in research, access to the central research library becomes more necessary. The fact that when the professors travel out from the base institution to the centers they can carry books from the main library with them doesn't really provide an adequate solution to the problem.

Old Shortcomings and New Experiments 95

For many, one of the most valuable aspects of living in a residential situation has been the opportunity for "bull sessions" in the dormitories with other students. <u>Can the extension seminary provide a substitute for this?</u> Not really. Something like the evening tea time in the pastor's house, as described in hypothetical center No. 3, is good, but not a real substitute for the warm fellowship and permanent friendships formed through the experience of a residential program. This is one reason we would not want to force an either-or choice between extension and residence. They both have things going for them, and we need them both.

<u>With the apparent skyrocketing of seminary enrollment because of extension, how do you expect the already short supply of teachers to keep pace?</u> This is not only a problem, it is a challenge, like needing more pews for your church. A partial answer is the fact that the use of teaching personnel is usually much more efficient in extension than in residence. One teacher can adequately handle many more students, since he meets with them only once a week instead of three times.

But it must be stressed that extension teaching is no pushover. It is an extremely demanding type of ministry. Not everyone is cut out for the discipline of traveling out week after week, sleeping in strange beds, eating what often turns out to be very humble fare, conversing until very late at night, and other difficult aspects of this new job. In our relatively short experience we have seen some put their hands to the plow and turn back, but many have adapted and gone on.

NEW EXPERIMENTS

Those who have given themselves to develop extension seminary training in recent years are well aware of the problems which have been mentioned, as well as others which may not have been mentioned. They are in a constant ferment to discover new ways to compensate for these shortcomings. The flexibility inherent in extension opens up innumerable possibilities for variation, many of which undoubtedly are waiting to be discovered and tried by some creative mind.

Predictably, the Guatemala pattern of extension has become the classic, the norm against which all else is measured. The new experiments are best described, therefore, as variations of the classical pattern. Some have been quite successful in their particular contexts, while some have not yet been adequately tested. Here is a list of some things that are being tried:

The monthly meeting. The Guatemala pattern prescribed a large gathering once a month of all the students in the seminary at the base institution. They felt this was important enough to subsidize, and the seminary would pay the travel costs of the students who came. But this was tried in the George Allan Seminary in Bolivia, and found unsuccessful. After just a few attempts, it was dropped. Among other things, the cultural, academic, and social gaps between urban folk studying at the bachelor level and rural folk studying at the certificate level were simply too great to allow any kind of meaningful joint program. If the program was geared for the rural folk, the urbanites stopped coming, and vice versa. In some places the monthly meeting has been discarded, in other places it continues.

Laymen's training. On the theory that theological subjects are not sufficiently learned unless they can be taught, some extension programs have built laymen's training into the courses themselves. In order to pass a course, say, on First Corinthians, the extension student must gather a group of five laymen and teach them on their level what he learns on his level. At the end of the course, the laymen are examined on First Corinthians, not by their student-teacher, but by the seminary professor in charge. If the five do not pass their exam, the student fails the course! This ties Christian education into theological education as little else which has been attempted to date. It does require a considerable increase in time and effort on the part of the professor who has one more thing to keep check on.

Less frequent visits. Some centers, such as the three Beni centers in Bolivia (San Antonio, Desengano, Santa Ana), are so far away from the base institution that air travel is the only reasonable way the professors could make regular visits. But due to the length of the flights, the high cost of each one, and the large block of professors' time consumed, it was evident that this could not be done every week. Bi-weekly visits were attempted although students in each one of the centers met together with a local leader weekly. Peter Savage, the professor involved, makes the following analysis: "Frankly, through many experiments, I have come back to the same conclusion that the regular weekly visit of the teacher is imperative for the effective systematic study of the student. I have found that students meeting the teacher every two weeks do approximately the same amount of work as the students meeting the teacher every week. Furthermore the rote learning system is so ingrained in them that many of the cognate skill areas such as analysis, synthesis, and application are not within their reach without the more frequent presence of the teacher."[2]

Short residence combined with extension. The same cluster of centers mentioned above in Bolivia's Beni area began their semester with what might have been the first floating extension seminary. Three river launches formed a fleet which spent two weeks on the winding rivers. During the day Professors Ingo Manhold and Philip Kavanagh held classes on board, then in the afternoons the launches would tie up at a port where the students would move out in a campaign of visitation, motion picture, and preaching evangelism. This was designed to bring the students together in a time of fellowship and cross-fertilization of thinking, get them off to a good start on their studies, and also relate their training to practical work. The report of this experiment indicates that "while the practical training was a success, there were serious limitations in the classroom studies."

Another variation of this experiment is being attempted in Oruro, Bolivia, where a semester's course begins with a week-long residence program, including specially invited teachers. It also finishes with a week-long residence, geared primarily toward evangelism and church planting. Most folk working in extension agree that if theological training does not result in growing churches, it is not fulfilling its basic purpose. To a degree, these attempts are alleviating some of the disadvantages of extension over against residence mentioned previously in this chapter.

Prolonged professor's visits. Raymond Morris, Vice-Rector of the George Allan Seminary in charge of rural training writes: "It has become evident that visits lasting two days or more are the most helpful among the Quechua brethren. At the same time, residence programs with them should not last longer than one week. We are now experimenting in some centers with two-month-long extension courses with two-day visits every three weeks. Shorter self-instructional books help the certificate level students set more attainable goals."[3]

Perhaps extending the weekly visits for a longer time in any of the extension programs would be worth investigating. For one thing it would help solve the problem of less teacher-student contact in extension than in residence. The average residence teacher may have six hours of classroom contact with his students and perhaps two more out of the classroom per week. If the extension professor could arrange to spend a whole day with his students, he could accumulate a larger weekly total of hours with them than the residence professor.

Concentrated courses. The programmed material that is used for extension can be adapted for use in a concentrated course of two or three weeks of residence where it is not yet possible to establish a classical extension center. If the students can spend six hours per day on one subject over a three-week period, they can complete the course just as if they had taken it over the normal fifteen-week extension period. Of course, the professor also must be in residence and meet with the students once a day instead of once a week. The important thing is that such a course would carry full credit in the seminary that offers it, thus distinguishing this training from what have been called in some places "laymen's institutes," really a form of *Christian* education in contrast to *theological* education.

Self-study extension-residence. Philip Kavanagh has run an experiment in the tropical area of Bolivia, the Beni, which merits some detail. He faced an almost insurmountable geographical problem. In the area around Magdalena, leaders from seven churches were selected by their regional denominational board as candidates qualified for extension training from the George Allan Seminary. But the area has no means of travel except horseback or oxcart, some of the churches being three or four days of travel from each other. Kavanagh's only option was air travel, but he in turn lived three air hours away from Magdalena in Cochabamba and was carrying a full schedule of residence courses. Furthermore, if he made each church a center he would have ended up with five centers with one student in each, and two with two students, hardly a good stewardship of a busy professor's time.

Since excellent programmed material had been produced on the level of the students, Kavanagh decided to try a self-teaching program without making use of the weekly visits. Once the students had enrolled he carefully worked out a timetable, and sent it to the students along with the materials via the mission pilot who was making an evangelistic tour through the region. Seven weeks later Kavanagh made his only visit to the "centers," where he checked on the progress of the students, examined them on the first twenty lessons, and found that they had progressed satisfactorily. At this writing, they have eight more weeks of self-study, then all nine will be flown to Magdalena for a three-week residence program. They will first be examined on the next 25 lessons of their course, and finish the final thirty lessons while in residence. At the same time they will be able to take another accredited course. An unaccredited course in Romans will also be offered in the evenings with interested church members invited, another happy combination of Christian education and theological education.

Curriculum modifications. Two changes in the ordinary curriculum are being attempted, one in Peru and one in Bolivia.

In Peru, Stewart McIntosh is developing perhaps the most radical experiment. He is designing a course with his sixteen extension students in Lamas which will allow them to finish the course and graduate in three years. In order to do this, he is eliminating courses not directly relevant to the particular type of ministry the students are already engaged in. They will receive a highly concentrated professional training, with heavy emphasis on the practical side. This has many apparent drawbacks, but it will be an experiment well worth watching.

In Bolivia, the George Allan Seminary is reorganizing its bachelor level course. Rather than carrying the normal curriculum of thirty semester-long subjects, all of which must be completed for graduation, the program is divided into three packages, each package terminating with graduation. The packages are: Basic Course (six subjects), Worker's Course I (twenty subjects), and Worker's Course II (twenty subjects). This is designed to give the student a feeling of accomplishment in shorter periods of time, reducing the possibility that the student will become discouraged with his work because of the unusually extended time between matriculation and graduation.

NOTES FOR CHAPTER 11

1. Ross Kinsler, *What is Extension?* mimeographed paper published as *Theological Monograph #3*, Theological Assistance Program of the World Evangelical Fellowship, October, 1970, p. 4.

2. Peter Savage in letter to Dr. Ted Ward, November 4, 1970.

3. Raymond Morris, "Report on Potosi Extension Department," *Minutes of the Meeting of the Board of Directors of the George Allan Theological Seminary*, October 13, 1970, translated from Spanish, p. 7.

12

EDUCATIONAL PRINCIPLES UNDERLYING EXTENSION EDUCATION

Two dangers threaten the educational validity of the extension seminary concept. The first is to view this approach to ministerial training as a glorified Sunday School class, a very inferior form of learning. It is fit, in this view, to be a Bible Institute program but does not rise to the dignity of a seminary. Extension training, so the argument goes, is the correspondence section of a "regular" seminary. Its graduates are not equal to the graduates of the traditional school, and thus they do not qualify for potential ordination.

A second danger is to compare the worst in the traditional seminary scheme with the best in the extension program. By this method, an educational millennium has arrived, and the only recourse is to dispense with past ways and wholeheartedly embrace the new.

Both of these extremes are to be avoided. The extension seminary does not offer an inferior education. It embodies valid educational principles which, when utilized rightly, afford the possibility of a more innovative education to more mature leaders than what is normally available on a resident campus.

TYPES AND LEVELS OF LEARNING

Teaching and learning are, unfortunately, not the same thing. If the source in the teaching-learning process in symbolized by (S), and the receptor is symbolized by (R) the intersecting portion of these two circles represents teaching that has resulted in learning $(S \cap R)$. The task of the good teacher is to increase the potential overlap of teaching that produces learning. Much research has been done on how animals and young children learn, but little is known about the learning process of adults. Furthermore, too little effort has been devoted on how to effectively relate teaching techniques to learning.

Learning has been defined as a change in behavior.[1] This behavioral change may be one of three types: (1) the psycho-motor, (2) the factual, and (3) the emotional. If the learning process is to be successful, i.e. attaining measurable goals, the teacher must clearly articulate which type of change is desired.

In some courses, the objective is to alter the pupil's emotional attitude. Most inner city internships or study programs seek to change the feeling which the student has toward ethnic minority groups. An effective course in Personal Evangelism will examine the student's attitude towards his own Christian experience, towards witnessing and towards those whom he seeks to win to Christ in order that these attitudes may conform to God's standards. If no attitudes have changed in such courses, then the educational objective has not been attained.

Some type of psycho-motor change is the goal of instruction in homiletics. Right habits of posture, proper use of hands, facial expressions suitable to the emotion expressed, and voice control are all training objectives. No amount of purely cognitive input will produce the physical control that is necessary. The student learns not merely what he should do, but he will be given practice in actually doing it.

Factual change by informational input is probably the most common goal of the educational process. Too often students conclude that this is the most important goal, or assume that to attain knowledge automatically results in psycho-motor or attitudinal change.

Learning defined more narrowly as cognitive input has five levels. Goals must be stated in terms of one of these levels if the learning output is to be properly evaluated. Let us state these concretely in terms of the chart in the ministry of the church in Chapter 2. The first level of cognitive input is *exposure*. The material is presented to illustrate a specific point. Learners are "exposed" to particular information, but there is no need for the material to be retained.

The second level is that of *recognition*. The student will recognize the drawing when he sees it a second time, although it probably will be presented in a slightly different context. The third level of cognitive learning is *recall*. Here the student will be able to recall the general configuration of the drawing, but he will not be able to reproduce verbatim all of the information that he has received.

The fourth level extends recall to *memory*. The learner will be able to reproduce exactly the drawing that the teacher has presented to him. Nothing will be omitted. The final and most complex learning level is the *concept* level. Here the student will be required to generalize among items that are similar, to discriminate closely between things that are different, and to transfer his learning into different situations. The latter ability is particularly critical. Little value will result from having memorized the drawing, if, when confronted by a specific need to analyze the situation in his own church, the student is not able to apply the essential concepts of the drawing to his local situation.

The actual content to be learned in any situation will depend upon the nature of the subject, priorities that the teacher established, and the levels of learning which are the objectives of the course.

Most learning processes will include a dynamic combination of psycho-motor, emotional, and cognitive change. Homiletics, again, may be an example. Certain physical abilities will have been mastered. The student will have overcome fear and learned how to establish emotional rapport with his audience. He understands the attitude necessary if an atmosphere for feedback is to be created. He has learned how to depend upon the Holy Spirit in sermon research, preparation and delivery. He is progressively developing a concern for people and their needs to which he addresses himself in his preaching. He also has learned a great deal about sermon construction, progression and sequence of thought patterns, and techniques of exegesis, exposition and topical sermon preparation. If any of these "changes" are lacking in his acquired behavior the sermon will not be fully effective.

TRADITIONAL EDUCATIONAL METHODS

What are the various ways in which cognitive input may be given? Broadly, these may be divided into the traditional and the progressive. Our primary concern is pragmatic and not theoretical, but traditional approaches have been associated with theories of mental discipline, and association, while progressive education is usually based upon theories of natural unfoldment, S-R connectionalism, reinforcement, and cognitive field.

What are some of the basic elements of traditional education? A lecture has been the long-established foundation of nearly all formal learning. The teacher has talked for most of the instructional period, and the student supposedly has been listening. The material presented by the lecture method may or may not be unique. Much of it may come from sources readily accessible to the student. It may include sequences of material and original research or insights not found in this combination in any printed material.

The lecture method has several weaknesses. If used extensively without other types of educational experience, the student is passive and lacks opportunity to participate actively in the learning process. Material that may be accessible to the student by reading is repeated unnecessarily in the class context. The lecture does not afford the student a learning model easily available to him for continuing education. This method is not the most efficient use of class time. No lecturer is able to talk as fast as his students can listen. Therefore, while he talks the potential learners are woolgathering. Present in body, they have long since departed in spirit and, with minds in neutral, they are mentally exploring more promising lands. If a fifty-minute lecture is recorded, and its milliseconds reduced by one-half through the shortening of syllables in a way that does not distort, its time is reduced to 25 minutes. When the student listens to this reduced version of the lecture, he is forced to "speed listen." His concentration is intensified, and the rate of his cognitive input is doubled. Further experiments are being made to even further increase the rate of input possible by this time-reduction of taped lectures.

Not that the lecture technique is completely negative in its impact. Much depends upon the personality of the teacher. If the presentation can stimulate the learner to "feel good," to reduce his fears while increasing his hopes, and to use various methods to reinforce the content being taught, learning will take place. Motivation is the critical factor. Older students with stronger goal orientation and better ability to relate even seemingly irrelevant material to life situations will not find the lecture so distasteful. Consequently, there will not be such a high degree of content absolescence.

Traditional pedagogy emphasizes the authority of the teacher. This implies not only his control of the teaching process, a factor to be desired, but also that the student must adjust to the teacher. Students are given little opportunity to participate, and their individual needs may be neglected. A given content to be imparted by a one-way communication process is emphasized over an inductive approach to truth.

In such a learning system major emphasis is placed on memory. Frenetic and compulsive note taking characterize the classroom experience, and little time remains for reflective thought. Too frequently, examinations are a regurgitation of ill-digested notes that have often been written in an illegible scrawl. Dr. Howard Hendricks of Dallas Theological Seminary tells the story of a student who rushed into his classroom at exam time, and, when the professor reached out to stop him for a moment, he frantically exclaimed, "Don't touch me, prof, or I'll leak!" He hurriedly sat down, took the exam sheet and quickly wrote down the mnemonic symbols that would jog his memory to answer correctly.

In countries of Asia, Africa, and Latin America such slavish slavery to memory is even more intense. Students will recite aloud together and read their notebooks audibly for hours on end to impress facts on their mind. Whatever else such stultifying memory procedures may accomplish, it is not to be equated with learning.

Traditional educational practice depends heavily upon extrinsic motivation of examination and recitation to promote learning. Little thought is given to factors of intrinsic motivation, of creating a learning situation where the student is motivated by his own needs, goals and the dynamism of the learning group.

PROGRAMMED INSTRUCTION

A more progressive method to furnish the cognitive input is to use self-instructional materials. The basic theory of such materials is well-known. The teacher, the programmed text in this instance, leads the student to make a response to a cognitive stimulus and then gives a variety of clues to increase the probability of the student making the same response each time a related stimulus is given. Right responses are reinforced, and wrong ones are extinguished. *[Behavior mod. Technique]*

Many types of programming techniques may be utilized. For illustrative purposes consider the following very simple frames where the student distinguishes between right and wrong answers and then constructs his own response.

    A. A Gospel is a Bible book which gives much factual detail about the earthly life of Jesus Christ. In the list below, place a check mark (✓) before each book that is a Gospel.

_____ 1. Mark   _____ 4. Luke

_____ 2. Romans   _____ 5. Acts

_____ 3. Revelation _____ 6. Galatians

* 1, 4

B. Place a check mark before each book that is a Gospel.

_____ 1. Philippians _____ 4. I Corinthians

_____ 2. Matthew   _____ 5. Hebrews

_____ 3. James   _____ 6. John

* 2, 6

C. Define a Gospel. Give two examples.

* A Gospel is a Bible book giving much detail about the life of Christ. Mark, Matthew

Note that the first frame has four sections: simple cognitive input; a problem; opportunity for response; immediate feedback. Correspondence courses and work books include the first three features. Feedback, however, in neither case is immediate, and this delay lessens the force of the reinforcement or extinction for the right or wrong answers respectively. The second frame eliminates the cognitive input, but it utilizes immediately the information from the first frame. The final frame requires the student to construct his answer from the previously given information. In each instance, the feedback is instantly available, but in a position on the page which discourages an honest person from cheating.

Although constructed on an elemental level, these frames utilize several educational principles basic to the way people learn.

1. New material is associated with old information. In a programmed sequence this series presupposes a previous one where the student has learned at least the names of various Bible books.

2. A clearly defined objective—to be able to write the definition of a Gospel—is built into this series. A good programmed textbook forces clarification of goals in measurable terms.

3. The goal is accomplished in several small steps, whose sequence has been carefully planned. This tends to increase motivation and interest.

4. Information is used as soon as it is presented.

5. A right response is immediately rewarded. This factor, so crucial to the learning process, is available to each student in a way not possible in the traditional classroom, even with more creative teaching techniques.

The discrimination and construction frames that have been illustrated here are types of a linear sequence where each student proceeds on a straight line through the frames. Another methodology, the branching frame sequence, routes the student through some common frames, but provides other sequences for students who have answered incorrectly. Theoreticians are quick to explain that the branching technique assumes that the student learns better by relating his mind to complex webs of information rather than to a simple one-to-one sequence of single bits of information.[2] Still other more sophisticated techniques, not yet utilized in extension seminary training texts, make it possible for one well-constructed textbook to meet the needs of students on different academic levels and from different cultural backgrounds.

Programmed instruction is closely related to the "stimulus and response" theory of learning and for this reason, some accuse it of being "behavioristic," thereby implying that it is a poor medium for communicating Christian truth. Two answers may be made to this objection: (1) Other theories of learning besides S-R also contribute to programmed learning; (2) Even if programmed learning has behavioral aspects, this does not necessarily imply that its view of man is behavioristic from either a philosophical or religious viewpoint.

It is important to realize that programmed instruction is only one facet of the total learning process utilized by the extension seminary. Ted Ward has observed that "current curriculum development reflect three characteristics: a) increasing use of field experiences, b) more variety in approaches to cognitive learning, and c) greater articulation between field experience and cognitive learning through seminars, symposiums and other forms of sharing experiences."[3] Dr. Ward compares items a) and b) to the upper and lower rail of a "split rail fence" and item c) to fence posts which function as a linkage between the two rails.

In the extension seminary, cognitive input comes through programmed instruction. The textbook is the real teacher. This releases the human teacher from the more traditional types of educational "house keeping." He has time to help the student, who ideally is a proven leader already involved in life situations in both the church and the world, to interpret his field experiences. Furthermore, he is a catalyst to help the student rightly interpret the cognitive input and relate this to his field experiences.

Extension seminary theory calls for weekly seminar sessions. High travel expense factors and difficult communication in large geographical areas may dictate bi-weekly or even monthly sessions lasting longer than a weekly meeting might. Such an approach has a foundation in theory. The optimum spacing of the seminar "fence posts" is not rigid. Ralph Winter uses the following diagram:

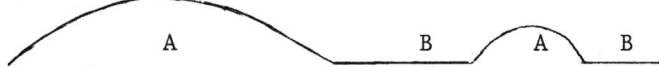

to pose the question "if 'A' represents the time of self-directed study and 'B' the time of teacher-contact, what is the ideal distribution of this time?"[4] The possibilities are infinite. "A" can represent one week and "B" one hour. Or "A" may be one month and "B" half-a-day. Or, as the C.M.A. are planning for an extension center in Saigon, "A" will be one month and "B" will be five one hour class sessions conducted on five successive days in one week. No educator is certain what spacing between these two types of experience will produce optimum results.

The extension seminary as defined within its development in the Latin American context is a new form of theological education. Its form is not yet stereotyped. This structural flexibility gives it great potential as a medium for these three elements of cognitive input, field experience and interpretative seminars, which Ward calls "an idealized model of the professional curriculum."[5]

NOTES FOR CHAPTER 12

1. James Espich and Bill Williams, <u>Developing Programmed Instructional Materials</u>, Palo Alto, Fearon Publishers, 1967, p. 4.

2. Ted Ward and Margaret Ward, <u>Programmed Instruction for Theological Education by Extension</u>, CAMEO, p. 33.

3. Ted Ward, *The Split Rail Fence: An Analogy for the Education of Professionals*, College of Education, Michigan State University, East Lansing, Michigan, p. 1.

4. Ralph Winter (ed.), <u>Theological Education by Extension</u>, William Carey Library, 1969, p. 157.

5. Ward, *Split Rail Fence*, p. 5.

13

THE INTERTEXT PROJECT AND ITS PROGRESS

By now it has become clear that programmed materials are even more than a cog in the wheel of the extension seminary--they are really the bearings that keep the whole machine running smoothly. Furthermore, preparing the programmed materials is by far the most difficult aspect of extension theological education.

The faculty of the Presbyterian Seminary in Guatemala deserve heroes' medals for accomplishing the gargantuan task of preparing a whole curriculum of materials for their seminary between the years 1962 and 1968. As Kinsler, Emery and Winter tell it now, those years of preparing the lessons week after week, living under the shadow of relentless, mind-crushing deadlines, writing and mimeographing programmed materials the whole night through to be ready to travel to the centers the next day, were the most difficult of their ministries from the standpoint of sheer labor.

Although the challenge of writing a programmed textbook that will be used to mold the minds of thousands of evangelical church leaders throughout Latin America would excite anyone to whom God has given a burden for theological education, not all who are working in extension seminaries should be assigned the responsibility. Not all can make the grade mentally or emotionally. I have seen the constant cumulative pressure bring programmers to the brink of a nervous breakdown. I have talked to wives utterly frustrated because their husbands are "married to that abominable programmed textbook." When you are teaching and programming at the same time, you soon find that you can't bluff your way through the weekly meeting like we all know we can through a lecture if for some reason we have not found time to prepare properly (Is this giving away a professional secret?). When you meet those students, you have to send them home with not one, but five, lessons ready for them to work on. There is no let up until the course is taught. Then the revision starts, because the first time through inevitably shows up innumerable weaknesses.

The first generation of Guatemalan materials had been prepared when the workshop met in Armenia, Colombia, in 1967. There a serious program designed to produce an entire theological curriculum in programmed form was launched. Few who attended realized how immense a task this would turn out to be. It was recognized that three essential elements had to be combined to accomplish the task: writers needed to be located, challenged with the opportunity, and provided with technical assistance. Publishers who would be willing to take on a rather unconventional operation had to be found and briefed. Finally a coordinated market needed to be established, a wide market which would give promise of economic feasibility, and also which would avoid duplication of efforts.

Which books needed to be written? The task of setting up a standard curriculum was one of the first objectives of the Armenia workshop. As curriculums from the various institutions represented were described and compared, it was found that a great deal of similarity existed among them. Before the workshop was over, a model curriculum had been established, and since then has met with quite wide acceptance on the continent. Some of the courses agreed upon are: History and Composition of the Old Testament; History and Composition of the New Testament; Genesis and Exodus; Jeremiah; Isaiah; Mark; Romans and Galatians; Church Growth; Evangelism; Social Ethics; Personal Ethics; Protestant Christianity in Latin America; Church Administration; History of Christianity; Christian Home; Pastoral Psychology; Anthropology; Homiletics; Pedagogy; Christian Education; Biblical Theology; and others. Since a book on each one of these courses is to be published on a pan-denominational basis, no general agreement was found as to whether it would be worthwhile to tackle a book on systematic theology, but some are still optimistic about the idea.

Once the matter of curriculum was settled, a level had to be established. The pioneers in Guatemala had projected multi-level programmed textbooks, but it was seen that this would not be an attainable short-range goal. Perhaps as experience built up, something that could be used by more than one level could be developed, but the problem of developing enough books to cover just the basic curriculum on only one level seemed big enough in itself. While the need for materials on every level was fully recognized, the unanimous consensus of the participants was that the project should begin on the diploma (post primary) level. The vast majority of the symbolic 100,000 church leaders who needed theological training were on the diploma level. This of course did not prohibit institutions from preparing their own materials on other levels, but it meant that the coordinated, international program would begin there.

A standardized structuring of the programmed books was the next item on the agenda. The academic year of 32 weeks was to be divided into sixteen-week semesters, fifteen weeks of study and one week of examinations. For each week five lessons or modules were to be written, each requiring about one hour of study on the particular academic level. With the weekly meeting a total of six study hours per week were required. This means that each programmed book would contain fifteen times five lessons, or a total of 75. If the particular course extended over two semesters, it would be based on 150 lessons.

The language of the Intertexts, as they began to be called, would have to be Spanish. One of the principles of programming is that the materials as much as possible should be prepared in the thought structure of the culture in which they will be used. The use of the Spanish language would best permit this to be accomplished. Perhaps other materials would be prepared in Portuguese in Brazil, but these could be translated without much difficulty, since the thought patterns are similar. The demand that some in the U.S.A. made that the Intertexts be written in English so they could be used on other continents was turned down. If others wanted to use them, they would have to translate them from the Spanish.

With these basic decisions made, it was decided that some sort of structure would have to be created to implement them. Those gathered knew ahead of time that any structure which was too formal or binding would never be accepted by the wide spectrum of churches the Intertext program hoped to serve. Instead of one strong, centralized committee, two very loosely organized committees were set up. One was called *Comite Latinoamericano de Textos Teologicos* (CLATT), and the other *Comite Asesor de Textos Autodidacticos* (CATA). My name was suggested to head up CLATT, and the late Wallace Rehner took charge of CATA.

As CLATT was organized, membership was not open to any and all. It was to be wide enough to include as full a geographical and denominational spectrum as possible, but narrow enough so that members could remain functional. The CLATT Secretary sent out invitations to several institutions asking them to join. Some accepted, some turned it down. As the present membership stands, it includes: Assemblies of God (representing their 23 Bible institutes in Latin America); Church of the Nazarene (which decided to join as an entire denomination); Baptist Theological Seminary, Bolivia; Baptist Evangelical Seminary, Argentina, (CBFMS); George Allan Theological Seminary, Bolivia (AEM/EUSA); Evangelistic Institute of Mexico; Alliance Bible Seminary, Ecuador, (C&MA); Latin American Bible Seminary, Costa Rica, (LAM); United Bible Seminary, Colombia, (OMS and others); Presbyterian Evangelical Seminary, Guatemala; and Contamana Bible Institute, Peru, (SAM).

Membership in CLATT indicates that the institution has a strong and active interest in extension theological education, that as much as possible it will provide authors to write programmed texts, that it will be kept informed of CLATT/CATA activities and offer suggestions to improve the program, that it will receive, read, make editorial recommendations, and if possible give approval to the preliminary edition of each Intertext before it is finally published. The name of each CLATT member institution which approves the Intertext will appear on the title page. It is hoped that the scrutiny of CLATT members will assure a thoroughly evangelical content in each Intertext, and will commend each one to as wide a range of churches in Latin America as possible.

The selection of authors was a very delicate and time-consuming process. CLATT and CATA worked closely together on this. Several who indicated their interest from the beginning have now fallen by the wayside, but others are continuing faithfully. It is hoped that eventually all the Spanish Intertexts will be authored by Latin Americans. At the present time this is not possible, so many missionaries are being used. Eventually, however, when a later generation of materials is produced, all will be written by those who have grown up with the language and thought patterns of the prospective students.

Some of the better-known names of authors in one stage or another of writing an Intertext are: Samuel Escobar (Social Ethics); Peter Savage (Biblical Theology); Ismael Amaya (The Work of Christ); Ross Kinsler (Jeremiah, Mark); Mary Savage (History and Composition of the Old Testament); James Emery (Pastoral Psychology); and many others.

The final responsibility of CLATT involves publishing the Intertexts as they are written and approved. Seven evangelical publishers, all of them well-known in Latin America have been contacted and have expressed their willingness to participate in the program. They are Moody Press, Caribe (Latin America Mission), Logoi, Spanish Baptist Publishing House, Nazarene Publishing House, Vida (Assemblies of God), and Las Americas

(Central American Mission). The general agreement is that these houses will handle the publication of the Intertext including customary author's royalties plus a 1 percent royalty to CLATT, and then distribute it through their regular distribution channels. Seminaries and Bible institutes will buy the Intertexts through bookstores or wholesale agents as they would any other text.

Before the publisher gets the manuscript, however, a preliminary edition will have been published in mimeographed or offset form by the institution to which the author belongs. The author and his institution agree beforehand to pay the cost of this and to airmail a copy of the preliminary edition to each CLATT member. They are also permitted to sell additional copies of the preliminary edition to other institutions, with the book being advertised in the regular CLATT bulletin. The official preliminary edition cannot be produced, however, until the CATA committee gives its approval.

Going back one step further in the publishing aspect, all editions which preceed the preliminary edition or which are done on levels other than the diploma level, are termed "stop gap" books. These also are advertised within the extension fraternity by CLATT and sold by the institution which produces them. The market for even stop gap materials is expanding. For example, in 1969 Raymond Morris' book on Personal Evangelism for the certificate level sold over 900 copies at $2.00 per mimeographed copy, and orders still are coming in for quantities of up to 100. Since this bypasses bookstores, it has been called "ad hoc publishing" to distinguish it from the "legitimate publishing" of the seven international publishing houses mentioned.

Whereas the role of CLATT is similar to that of a literary agent in working with authors, publishers, contracts, markets, etc., that of CATA is more specialized and technical. This committee, now coordinated by Ross Kinsler, with James Emery, Peter Savage, and Wayne Weld as regional secretaries, controls the quality of the programming itself. They are concerned, not so much with what the book contains (as are the CLATT folk), but whether the book, after all, will *teach*. Since the book replaces the traditional lecturer, it must be good. CATA sees that the authors, some of whom know nothing about programming when they begin, get the proper orientation at the beginning and sound advice along the way.

One of the most useful tools for accomplishing this purpose has been the programming workshop. Ross Kinsler and Peter Savage have held several of these, and they have brought in

The Intertext Project and Its Progress 115

outsiders such as Ted Ward of Michigan State University. Skeptical of the program at first, Ward, a conservative evangelical, is now one of its most convinced advocates. Growing out of a number of workshops he held with CLATT authors and their counterparts in Brazil, was his timely book called <u>Programmed Instruction for Theological Education by Extension</u>.[1] Now that this is available, anyone with a good grasp of his subject and average pedagogical aptitude, can begin programming by following the instructions of this book along with the two other books it recommends, Espich and Williams, <u>Developing Programmed Instructional Materials</u>,[2] and Mager, <u>Preparing Instructional Objectives</u>.[3]

The regional secretaries of CATA make it a habit to get together with the authors assigned to them every few months, either by traveling to the author's home or vice-versa. By doing this, they have helped avoid serious errors which would result in much futile work later to be rejected by CATA. A flow chart, 64 inches long, and including 41 separate stages of development has been prepared by CATA in both Spanish and English, and is used with each author. Built into the process are four tests previous to acceptance of the Intertext as a preliminary book, and one between that time and the time it is finally revised for publication. The first four include: "Sample worked by informant in presence of author" (Stage 16); "One or two sections prepared and presented to regional secretary" (Stage 18); "Sample testing with individuals or group" (Stage 29); and "Field test performed by author" (Stage 32). A failure at any one of these points means another complete revision of the material before it can go to the CLATT members.

Twice CATA has sponsored large, international meetings gathering together those actively involved in the program, seriously evaluating mistakes and shortcomings, brainstorming for creative ideas for the future, and reorganizing when necessary. The first of these was held in Mexico City in December, 1968, and the second in Bogota, November, 1969. The third will probably be held sometime in 1971.

Only one Intertext has gone into its preliminary edition, <u>Principles of Church Growth</u> by Wayne Weld and Donald McGavran. Immediately after it was approved by CATA, the preliminary edition was air mailed to the CLATT members. Eight of the eleven have examined it and accepted it, the other three have not responded. Moody Press has published "Intertext No. 1" with the names of the approving CLATT institutions appearing on the title page. With this book now on sale it is the beginning of a dream come true, and the first fruits of three years of labor on the part of those who have dedicated a large share of their ministries to the CLATT/CATA Intertext program.

While the CLATT/CATA project got underway in Spanish-speaking Latin America, in Brazil a similar program was taking shape. Ralph Winter held a theological education workshop in Sao Paulo in August, 1968 where 23 seminaries and Bible institutes were represented by 55 participants. This workshop stimulated enough interest for the Brazilians to call and organizational meeting of the *Associacao Evangelica Teologica para Treinamento por Extensao* (AETTE). Peter Savage represented CATA at that meeting, held in October of 1968. The Brazilians have seen fit to organize just one committee to control all extension education in the country, and have elected Richard Sturz of the Conservative Baptists as its head. In April, 1969, another workshop was held on curriculum and programming, again led by Peter Savage, who has been the liaison man between CLATT/CATA and AETTE through the years.

Interchange between the Spanish and Portuguese programmed materials is not anticipated before the final Intertext stage. When Intertexts are published, it is expected that the majority of them will be translated into the cognate language and used in extension on the other part of the continent.

NOTES FOR CHAPTER 13

1. Ted and Margaret Ward, <u>Programmed Instruction for Theological Education by Extension</u>, Denver, CAMEO, 1970.

2. J. E. Espich and Bill Williams, <u>Developing Programmed Instructional Materials</u>, Palo Alto, Fearon Publishers, 1967.

3. R. F. Mager, <u>Preparing Instructional Objectives</u>, Palo Alto, Fearon Publishers, 1962.

14
THE THIRD STAGE IN AFRICA AND ASIA

Workshops held in the summer of 1970 in eight countries of Asia and Africa represent the third stage of the extension seminary rocket. Blast-off came in Latin America, first with the initial program in Guatemala and then through a series of workshops in 1967-68 in Colombia, Ecuador, Bolivia, and Brazil which rapidly communicated the concept to most of the subcontinent. The rocket went into a parking orbit preparatory to even further extension with two significant meetings in 1968 at Philadelphia and Wheaton, which introduced the idea to missionaries from non-Latin American countries.

As these missionaries returned to their spheres of overseas service, the climate was created for "grass-root" extension seminary workshops in Asia and Africa. Missionaries liked what they had heard at Philadelphia and Wheaton, but was it a Latin American phenomenon? Could this revolutionary idea be exported? CAMEO was willing to help them find the answer. Funds were obtained from the National Liberty Foundation, resource personnel were selected, and coordinators in the target countries were authorized to arrange details for the workshops.

Ted Ward and Sam Rowen conducted workshops in Ethiopia, Nigeria, Rhodesia, and Kenya. The fellowship was warm, but the high countries of Africa in August can be cold, and Dr. Ward suggested that CAMEO may wish to send Eskimos as its representatives on the next trip! Asia in August is *not* cold and the two resource personnel, Peter Wagner of the Andes Evangelical Mission and Ralph Covell of the Conservative Baptist Seminary in Denver, perspired their way through two workshops in Taiwan, one each in Vietnam, Indonesia and India, and a short consultation with church and mission leaders in Singapore.

The leadership crisis in Africa is similar to that in Latin America. The church is growing rapidly and training programs cannot keep pace with it.[1] The majority of the present pastors have not had a secondary school education. They are badly overworked, often assuming responsibility for as many as fifty congregations. Most African pastors function as "tent makers," supporting themselves by farming with only minimal financial help from their congregations.[2]

Techniques integral to the development of an extension seminary program, such as self-instructional materials, are being introduced by secular educators in sub-Sahara Africa. No theoretical obstacles are envisaged which would hinder such materials from gaining wide acceptance as a valuable teaching tool.[3]

Techniques aside, the *concept* of extension education may not be welcomed by Africans. Education and status are so integrally related that any program appearing to be outside the normal system may not be viewed either as educationally valid or sufficiently prestigious. Years of immersion in patterns of Western education make it difficult to separate learning from acquisition of facts. This tendency to prize correct answers rather than methods of learning caused students in Nigeria to cheat their way through programmed materials by looking first at the answers.[4]

Given these needs and the in-built problems, how did Ward and Rowen approach their task? First, they carefully laid a foundation in theory to support the superstructure of extension training. Institutional goals, curriculum building, the danger of Westernisms, the function of teachers and the peer group in the learning process were among the topics discussed. Delegates wondered "when are they going to talk about the extension seminary?" but finally realized that these workshops would have failed if merely consisting of "how-to-do-it" sessions.

In the second place, teaching techniques characteristic of extension methodology were used in the workshops to give the "cognitive input." While lectures were utilized, more emphasis was placed upon simulation models of both church growth and decentralized training, of discussion and of actual delegate participation in stating goals and in programming materials. Delegates differed in their information about and their commitment to extension training. Therefore, during half of each workshop day Ward gave intensified instruction to those wishing to write programmed materials, while Rowen led more general seminars on extension seminary concepts.

How did the resource personnel evaluate the present and potential results of these conferences? Of major importance was that attitudes toward the purpose of theological education were clarified and sharpened. Many delegates had elementary experience in material preparation. They have a clearer understanding of who is able to do what in programs being projected. For the first time church and missionary educators and administrators see potential answers to their perplexing problem of training church leaders.

More specifically, actual implementation of the new ideas was begun. In Ethiopia this meant no more than to form a very loose *ad hoc* committee responsible to develop plans for an organizational structure through which to exchange information and implement mutually agreeable plans on extension education. Delegates at the Nigeria workshop decided to call for a workshop on Programmed Instruction as soon as possible and to experiment in extension programs during the school vacation period. At least two schools represented at the Rhodesia conference fully or partly phased out resident programs by the end of 1970 and commenced extension training.

An ever present danger at each workshop was the pressure to institutionalize results in some type of continuing organization. To have done this would have been unfortunate for several reasons. First, it could have created rigid structures before there had been sufficient local discussion, particularly with national leaders who were not always well represented. Second, it would have excluded representatives from both non-attending EFMA-IFMA groups and from attendants belonging to non-EFMA, non-IFMA bodies. Third, it would have imposed an organization from above rather than allowing it to develop from the needs of each separate situation. The resource personnel wisely separated themselves from this decision-making level by African churches and mission societies.[5]

The church in Asia, except in those societies which are largely animistic, is not growing rapidly.[6] The yawning gap between numbers of churches and leaders-in-preparation is not nearly so great in much of Asia as in Africa and Latin America. Bruce Nicholls, theological coordinator for the World Evangelical Fellowship and a professor at the Union Biblical Seminary in Yeotmal, observes that "unless there is a revival in India and rapid church growth, we may reach a saturation point in the number of full-time fully paid pastors."[7]

Meanwhile, the concept of "full-time, fully paid pastors" is the generally accepted pattern for the ministry. Unwisely imported North American and European concepts of the ministry account for some of this sense of ministerial status. An even larger contribution derives from the hierarchical nature of Confucian philosophy and the Indian *gurukula* ideal, both of which stress the high status of the specialist teacher who imparts information. In fact, within the many societies influenced by Chinese culture, the word for "church" literally means the "teaching society," and the pastor is a religious version of the Confucian teacher.

Theoretically, the Confucian model and the *gurukula* ideal, in initial conception and historic development, commonly possess features upon which the extension concept could build: apprenticeship training, close master-disciple relationship, strong goal orientation (government service via examination on the Confucian classics), tutoring, and training diffused in rural communities. Unfortunately, it is the scholarly image, emphasis upon memorization of theoretical and classical information, and the sense of status which have had the most pervasive influence upon Christian education.

Some features of the general educational scene in various Asian countries could reinforce concepts of extension education. Teachers on the secondary level in Vietnam are encouraged to continue their own study permanently. Schools are being taken to the adult in a plan modeled on that of Israel.[8] A variety of extension courses in many subject areas are being developed by the colleges and universities of India.[9] A pilot project was held at Bombay and Poona from January to April, 1970, to evaluate the potential of Programmed Instruction for Indian education.[10] The Soka Gakkai in Japan have involved 1,173,437 people on six levels--professors, associate professors, assistant professors, associate assistant professors, lecturers, and assistant lecturers--in a massive program of decentralized lay education.[11] Innovative plans of apprenticeship training have been used in some churches in Celebes, Indonesia.[12]

The Asian workshops were more lecture-oriented than those in Africa, although each presentation was followed by extensive discussion, often lasting longer than the original lecture. The need for translation into national languages in three of the five workshops would have made simulation models very difficult. Each evening and the entire final day of every workshop were spent in small group discussions for local planning and implementation.

Each meeting had its own dynamism. Two of the five workshops were, in Peter Wagner's words, "evangelistic"--geared to persuade delegates that extension education was a valid option for ministerial training. Three represented "follow-up"--

further explanation of how decentralized theological education could fit the needs of local situations.

What happened at these workshops?

In Taiwan, the conclusion was reached that the new cooperative graduate theological school, China Evangelical Seminary, would serve as the constituting organization for proposed extension outreach that ultimately would teach students on three academic levels--college graduates, upper high school graduates, and lower high school graduates. A committee was formed to plan an organizational structure, to draw up a tentative curriculum, and, if feasible, to assign writers to prepare self-teaching materials. During the 1970-71 academic year China Evangelical Seminary has conducted extension training for five students in the evenings.

The next Asian workshop was conducted in the facilities of the International Church in Saigon. The eighty participants were largely missionaries and church leaders from the Christian and Missionary Alliance, the largest Protestant denomination in Vietnam. During the four-day conference presentations were made by the resource personnel on the philosophy of extension education, the biblical foundation of theological education in the nature of the church and its ministry, varying historical forms of theological education, models of ministerial training in various Latin American countries, the processes of learning and curriculum development. A summary statement issued by church and mission personnel at the concluding service recommended the development of extension theological education in Vietnam to meet the following areas of need:

1. Training of church leaders for tribal areas about Dalat and Ban Me Thuot.

2. Continuing education for pastors.

3. Training of urban church leaders in centers such as Saigon.

The third Asian workshop was held in the headquarters of the Inter-Mission business office in Djakarta, Indonesia. This gathering included 47 delegates from thirteen different groups. The geographical spread was awesome with representatives from West Irian, Sumatra, Kalimantan, Java, Timor, Ambon, Celebes, Malaysia, and Singapore. Some had travelled as far as 2,000 miles to be present. Groundwork preparation had been done well by several of the groups, resulting in an unusually receptive attitude to extension concepts. A unique difficulty to the establishing of extension centers in Indonesia will be lack of adequate land and sea transportation. Fortunately, the recently developed ministry of Missionary Aviation Fellowship encouraged delegates to feel that this obstacle could be overcome at reasonable expense. The value of extension seminary education was seen to be two-fold: to stimulate church growth through many more trained church leaders and to "up grade" many poorly trained leaders in existing churches.

Two basic decisions were reached at this workshop.

1. To form an *ad hoc* organizing committee of three to coordinate continuing efforts and to suggest a structure for a united program in extension theological training.

2. To request CAMEO to arrange for translation into English of selected Spanish materials used in Latin America theological education. This request, although only formally articulated in Indonesia, was a frequently voiced desire in each area where workshops were held.

The final workshop was held at Union Bible Seminary at Yeotmal, Central India. Fifty-five delegates from fifteen groups were present from nearly all of the geographical areas of India and came prepared to implement a united extension seminary program on a nationwide scale. A decision was reached to form a working committee of ten that would prepare a constitution for a Theological Extension Association comprised of all existing seminaries and Bible institutes that wish to participate.

In all of these workshops several types of emphases were needed to remove misunderstandings in the minds of many participants. The first emphasis was that extension education aims to extend and thus complement existing training institutions rather than to eliminate them. The second was that extension education is, at the very least, equally as valid a learning process as that used in the more traditional training programs and thus will not result in an inferior ministry. The third was that each national church must itself determine how the students trained at many different levels will fit into its ministry. Questions of accreditation and ordination always lurked behind the discussions on theological education. The fourth was that extension education can function both as a means to train many more leaders needed to minister in areas of rapid church growth and as a method to train large numbers of evangelists to promote church growth. The fifth was that decentralized training can give men a good theological education even on the sixth grade level!

Two problems were difficult to resolve. First, many of the national participants viewed extension education as a threat to their status. Trained in existing schools and serving as full-time, fully paid pastors, they were reluctant to accept any alternative pattern that would make it "easy" for large numbers of "laymen" to be equal with them! The "tent-making ministry" is not a common pattern with many groups. The tradition of formal education is deeply rooted. As soon as it became apparent that extension training could first be used to upgrade the present pastorate in continuing education a good deal of the suspicion and resistance was removed.

Second, how can extension education, largely "word" oriented, be implemented among many tribal groups, who at best, are not functionally literate? In what ways can audio-visual materials be used to solve this difficult problem? Do people have to be literate before their gifts of leadership can be developed? Answers to these questions are crucial if extension education is to be properly implemented in many parts of Indonesia, Vietnam and India.[13]

Two distinct advantages for the implementation of extension training in Asia are COFAE--The Coordinating Office for Asian Evangelism--and the presence in Asia of Bruce Nicholls, theological coordinator of the World Evangelical Fellowship, and Dr. Athayal, Asian theological coordinator of W.E.F. Dr. Athayal, Professor Nicholls, and Bishop Ray, Director of COFAE, helped to plan the Asia Evangelical Theological Consultation held in Singapore, July 5-7, 1970, at which time extension education and many other facets of theological training were discussed.[14]

The existence of such ready-made structures, the availability of well-known leaders, and the experience gained through Pacific area conferences of the type held in Singapore provide a regional unity and a spirit of cooperation which speaks well for the development of truly Asian programs and methods of theological education by extension.

NOTES FOR CHAPTER 14

1. Dr. McGavran quotes the missionary principal of a seminary in Africa who reports that his church has only fifty adequately trained ministers for 609 churches and that only nine men are being graduated and ordained each year. Ralph O. Winter (ed.), Theological Education by Extension, Pasadena, 1969, xiii.

2. Douglas Webster, "A Time for Honesty About the Ministry," *International Review of Missions*, 52, October, 1963, pp. 385-398.

3. Gerald Bates, *The Extension Seminary--Its Potential for Africa's Young Churches*, Seminar paper, Michigan State University, June, 1970, p. 6.

4. Scott B. Parry, "What the West Africans Taught Us About P. I.," *Programmed Instruction*, Vol. 4, April, 1965.

5. The material on the African workshops has come from reports by Ted Ward, Sam Rowen, and the local coordinators. These are all included in a compilation on the African and Asian workshops distributed by CAMEO in October, 1970.

6. Korea with its predominant Shamanism would be included here. See Roy Shearer, Wildfire: Church Growth in Korea, Grand Rapids, Eerdmans, 1966, pp. 30-31.

7. Bruce J. Nicholls, *Theological Education in India*, p. 5.

8. Message at Saigon workshop by Prof. Vu Duc Chang. See also *School Comes to Adults Israel*, paper presented to the World Congress of Ministers of Education on the Eradication of Illiteracy, Teheran, 1965.

9. I. N. Thut and Don Adams, Educational Patterns in Contemporary Societies, New York, McGraw Hill, 1964, pp. 417-420.

10. Phil C. Lange and Desmond P. Wedberg, "The Feasibility of Programmed Learning for Developing Countries," *Audio-Visual Instruction*, April, 1970, pp. 65-67.

11. James Dator, Soka Gakkai, Builders of the Third Civilization, University of Washington Press, 1969, p. 144.

12. Reports at Djakarta workshop by Dave Moore of the C.M.A. on the KIBAID school started by Mr. Bokko in Toradja, p. 2.

13. The only book that really deals with this type of problem at present is Hans Ruedi Weber, <u>The Communication of the Gospel to Illiterates</u>.

14. Expanded minutes of the *Asia Evangelical Theological Consultation*, Singapore, 5-7, July, 1970.

15

THE EXTENSION SEMINARY AND CHURCH GROWTH

The primary thrust of the extension seminary is to extend the church of Jesus Christ. To extend the seminary geographically, culturally, economically, and academically to fit the needs and capabilities of the student without the church being multiplied will be to fail.

The goal of mission activity is not to develop a new and more effective system of theological education but to fulfill the Great Commission--the quantitative and qualitative growth of the church. The value of extension training awaits the verdict of history--at least a ten or fifteen-year period during which time a careful analysis must be made of the actual church growth that has occurred.

In the provision of God such a "breakthrough" in leadership development could not have come at a more opportune time. The church of Jesus Christ in Africasia is at the threshold of unprecedented advance. All previous mission history pales in significance before the dimension of today's potential. The church in Latin America is growing at the rate of 10 percent annually, well beyond the 3 percent rate of natural population increase.[1] David Barrett predicts, on the basis of a careful statistical analysis, that the church in Black Africa will constitute 57 percent of the total population below the Sahara by A.D. 2000.[2] The cyclic pattern of the advance and recession of the church of Christ noted by Dr. Latourette will no longer be determined solely by the state of the church in Europe and North America.[3] These areas will slip into the limbo of relative insignificance, while the center of the Christian movement will move to "the younger churches," particularly the church in Africa.

God has laid the burden of evangelism upon his people worldwide. Sparked by the Berlin Congress on Evangelism in 1966, regional and national conferences on evangelism have been held in the United States, Africa, Latin America and Asia. During 1970 alone conferences on evangelism have met in India, Thailand, the Philippines, Taiwan and in the United States for the Latin American population. A saturation evangelism campaign was held in Shikoku, Japan, a spirit of revival and evangelism has continued in Indonesia, and an intensive Evangelism-Deep-and-Wide program is gaining momentum in Vietnam.[4]

How can the extension seminary contribute to this growth? Three possibilities are most apparent. Extension programs will train the leaders who have come to the surface in these rapidly multiplying congregations. New churches will die or turn toward heresy without adequately trained leaders. The extension seminary will train leaders from static churches to be the evangelists in programs of new outreach. Finally, this method of decentralized training will afford new opportunities for pastors to "upgrade" their education and to feel more confident in facing the challenges of the present day which demand new forms for the church and its ministry.

It would be easy for today's strategists to be messianic in their emphasis and gratuitously assume that theological education has never produced church growth. Mission history reveals repeated examples of innovative and functional forms that Christ has used to build his Church. The apprentice method characterizing the primitive church and the Methodist movement in both England and the United States stands out. The Ruanda scheme used by the Church Mission Society integrates periods of study and church involvement, rewarding those who showed academic ability, spiritual growth, and gifts of ministry with opportunity for further study and work advancement.[5] The Chilean Pentecostal Church has trained its pastors "on the street." Promotion depended upon measurable spiritual productivity.

The Assemblies of God Bible School in San Salvador, El Salvador, has maximized practical work, often demanding that students evidence their ability to plant churches before they can complete their academic training program. Many mission groups and national churches periodically hold short-term Bible schools, evening classes, or a variety of special training programs, all of which are semi-extension and aim to upgrade every level of present church leadership for a diversity of ministries. Some traditional programs of theological education emphasize proven principles of church growth. We would be blind either not to note these noteworthy efforts or to assume that they are the rule rather than the exception.

Static traditionalism is the normal pattern in overseas theological education and has tended to inhibit the extension of the church. The widespread interest in extension education is a measure of the dissatisfaction felt. Dr. McGavran has observed that one of the basic points of "church growth" philosophy is that "theological education should be revamped so that seminaries graduate many men successful in church planting."[6] Why this need for revamping? Where are the problems? In what specific ways may the extension seminary, if properly implemented, serve as a corrective?

Traditional seminary programs *extract* men from their natural environment in the world and insulate them from real life situations. The "ghetto mentality" produced by this artificial learning situation reinforces the concept of the church as a place to which the world is to come rather than as a staging base from which it penetrates the world. Inflexible attitudes are developed in training with little possibility of adjustment to the changing forms of ministry and church planting demanded, for example, by burgeoning urban regions like Hong Kong, Saigon, and Calcutta. If the seminary does "business as usual" its graduates will only engage in church housekeeping. A less institutionalized seminary training may help future pastors see the viability of flexible forms of ecclesiastical life--the house church, for example.

Furthermore, the "leader-to-be" is separated from his own people and may find it difficult to return to them, particularly if they are in a rural area or from a cultural minority group. The graduate from such a program has the status of a semi-professional. He has gone away to school and now qualifies to move into the elite leadership of the church. He must have a role equal to his attainment. The Hakka populace of Taiwan has been deprived of all potential for the planting of new churches, since the young Hakka men sent to Taipei or Tainan for training in two major Presbyterian seminaries have settled down in more convenient pastorates among the Taiwanese. Would this have happened if they had been trained in the Hakka areas?

Even where graduates do return to their original homes for service it may be with attitudes that make it difficult for them to serve effectively. Dr. George Vicedom recommended that the Yuli Theological Institute on the East Coast of Taiwan be decentralized to better meet the needs of students studying there from the ten tribal groups.[7] Sheer idealism and totally impractical for a traditional seminary program was the verdict, and his advice was rejected with the consequent loss in growth potential. His suggestion could easily have been implemented by the concept of extension.

Training by extraction is expensive. Heavy subsidy is the name of the game. The student--usually a young man with no job and with no secular vocational experience--develops a spirit of dependence. As the seminary has supported him with mission funds, perhaps creating a token campus job for him, so will the mission continue to support him after graduation. Thus a system of subsidized church pastors is created which limits church extension to the availability of outside resources. Furthermore, the only viable pattern within this system will be the "full-time" pastor. The extension seminary creates the possibility of another pattern--a temporary or permanent "part-time" ministry. If a man has been trained while making his living in the world, he will not need to be weaned from mission funds nor will he find it demeaning to his status to continue along the same path.

Training by *extraction* is never certain whether or not it has a product. The students may or may not become leaders; they may or may not have Spirit-given gifts for leadership. The attrition rate before graduation is 30-40 percent, but, even more tragic, the only thing we know for sure about those who remain is that they can get passing grades! Can they produce in the work of Christ? The extension seminary trains more mature men already working in churches. They will produce because they are producing. They are leading men and exercising the gifts given to them for ministry by God the Holy Spirit.

Some extension programs radically emphasize leadership development. The Honduras Extension Bible Institute, run by C.B.H.M.S., is calling those who study "worker" rather than "student." Courses are highly functional. The one which introduces the New Testament is called "Communication of the New Testament." The goal of the institute is "to equip and mobilize dedicated workers to carry on by themselves immediately the spiritual production both of individual Christians and of churches."[8]

Culture in most areas of the world is a mosaic with a number of homogeneous groups. Church growth will best be promoted by training leaders from each group where there are churches or where church planting is projected. Training by extraction is a "melting pot" approach. Differences are minimized with little allowance for the variety of backgrounds represented in the student body. Under pressures to develop a unified curriculum and methodology, no creative thought can be devoted to preparing the student to meet the specific needs of his particular cultural group. Potentialities and possibilities of various church growth patterns are overlooked by the cultural levelling process of the educational approach. The extension seminary is better able to develop multi-cultural curriculums and to utilize "on-the-spot" training to stimulate creative student response to their own cultures.

The traditional seminary program can inhibit church growth by preparing leadership on only one or two levels. Concentration is usually on the middle-class student who may be ill-prepared either to reach the lower classes (the so-called "masses" of church growth theory) below him or the intellectual classes above him. Efficiency of operation, centralized location, common classes and other factors dictate concentration on one or two levels with the result that the needs of the entire church are not fully met. The extension seminary can do a good job of education for ministry on several academic levels. It trains the men whom God has equipped, irrespective of their educational backgrounds. Ralph Winter observes that an "unexpected discovery" of the extension program of the Evangelical Seminary in Guatemala was that "extension centers allowed us to reach up to higher as well as down to lower academic levels than we had operated on before."[9]

A warning is necessary at this point. Extension training is the "in" thing. Everyone wants to get on the bandwagon. Any kind of an effort, as long as it tips its hat to the name "extension," is seen as a panacea for every ill of the church. Many half-hearted programs, with ill-conceived materials, and giving no academic credit to a potpourri of students, lumped together in "catch-all" lay-training courses, are being dignified as extension training. Little wonder that some church leaders are adverse to granting ordained status in their churches to such ill-prepared leaders. Dr. Winter cautions that extension can go wrong if it loses sight of the "primary goal of the early proponents of theological education by extension which is to reach out to the real pastoral leadership of the church with first rate theological education that will allow these men of high potential to become more than second-class leaders."[10] First-rate extension training will gradually diminish status consciousness among church leaders and increasingly make it possible for churches to ordain men trained by extension as well as those who have graduated from the more traditional schools.

No observation came more frequently in Asia from workshop delegates than this critical one, "Our churches are not growing and we have enough leaders at present. Are extension methods as necessary then for us as in Latin America?" This very statement misses the point that the extension seminary can train men gifted in evangelism for massive new outreach with the Gospel. Vast, untapped resources are to be found in "God's frozen people." Here is the army that can penetrate a world for Christ. Many of them will never be reached in our traditional seminaries. And as long as we put all our eggs in the *extraction* basket we will limp along with only a very small portion of the resources God has given his church.

The church must grow qualitatively in biblical knowledge, in Christian piety, and in many forms of dedicated service. Pastors long for renewed learning opportunities. If they must leave their sphere of ministry and go away to school, both quantitative and qualitative growth will suffer. How far superior to train them where they are as they continue to serve Christ.

The extension seminary and church growth? In a nutshell, decentralized theological education enables us to prepare more and better leaders on a variety of levels and from a variety of homogeneous cultural units. These men will take places of innovative leadership within rapidly multiplying new churches and spearhead evangelistic outreach into whitened harvest fields.

NOTES FOR CHAPTER 15

1. William Read, Victor Monterroso, and Harmon Johnson, *Latin American Church Growth*, Eerdmans, 1969, p. 55.

2. David R. Barrett, "A.D. 2000: 350 Million Christians in Africa," *International Review of Mission*, Vol. 59, January, 1970, pp. 39-54.

3. Kenneth Latourette, *The Unquenchable Light*, New York, 1941, is a brief presentation of this thesis.

4. *In-Depth Evangelism Around the World*, Office of Worldwide Evangelism-in-Depth, Latin American Mission, Miami, Florida, Sept.-Oct., 1970 issue, pp. 1-4.

5. Donald McGavran, *How Churches Grow*, London, 1959, pp. 140-1.

6. Donald McGavran. From a summary entitled, "Ten Prominent Elements in the Church Growth Point of View" and included in an article, "What McGavran's Church Growth Thesis Means," *Evangelical Missions Quarterly*, Volume 3, Fall, 1966, p. 23.

7. Report from George Vicedom to the Board of Missions of the Presbyterian Church in Canada, 1958.

8. James Clark and George Patterson, "Honduras Extension Bible Institute," *Missions Reference Library*, C.B.H.M.S., pp. 12-30.

9. Ralph D. Winter, (ed.), *Theological Education by Extension*, William Carey Library, S. Pasadena, Calif., 1969, pp. 307-8.

10. Ralph D. Winter, "A Revolution Goes Into Orbit," *World Vision Magazine*, Volume 14, November, 1970, p. 15.

BIBLIOGRAPHY

Asia Evangelical Theological Consultation, Expanded Minutes, Singapore, July 5-7, 1970.

Barrett, David R., "A.D. 2000: 350 Million Christians in Africa," *International Review of Missions*, Vol. LIX, January, 1970, pp. 39-54.

Bates, Gerald, *The Extension Seminary, Its Potential for African Young Churches*, mimeographed paper, Lansing, Michigan State University, 1970, 13 pp.

Bradshaw, Malcolm R., "Theological Education," *The Way*, No. 2, 1970, Singapore, IFES.

Bruce, A. B., The Training of the Twelve, Edinburgh, T. & T. Clark, 1908.

Chang, Prof. Vu Duc, address at Saigon, Viet Nam, Extension Workshop, 1970.

Clark, James and George Patterson, "Honduras Extension Bible Institute," *Missions Reference Library*, C.B.H.M.S., pp. 12-30.

Coleman, Robert E., The Master Plan of Evangelism, New York, Revell, 1964.

Dator, James, Soka Gakkai, Builders of the Third Civilization, University of Washington Press, 1969, p. 144.

Daube, David, The New Testament and Rabbinic Judaism, London University of London, 1956, pp. 206,16.

Bibliography

Dodd, Charles, *The Apostolic Preaching and Its Developments*, New York, Harper, 1936, p. 26.

Emery, James H., "The Preparation of Leaders in a Ladino-Indian Church," *Practical Anthropology*, Vol. 10, No. 3, 1963, pp. 127-134.

Espich, James and Bill Williams, *Developing Programmed Instructional Materials*, Palo Alto, Fearon Publishers, 1967.

Hay, Alexander, *The New Testament Order for Church and Missionary*, Buenes Aires, Argentina, New Testament Missionary Union, 1947, Supplement to Chapter IV.

Hodges, Melvin L., "The Selection of Ministerial Candidates," *Church Growth Bulletin, Volumes I-V*, Donald A. McGavran, ed., South Pasadena, William Carey Library, 1969, p. 232.

Hopewell, James, "Mission and Seminary Structure," *International Review of Missions*, Vol. 56 (April, 1967), p. 158.

Horne, H. H., *Jesus the Master Teacher*, Grand Rapids, Kregel, 1968.

James, W. Paul, "Action Training and the Seminaries: Four Possibilities," *Theological Education*, Winter, 1970, pp. 152-159.

Jeremias, Joachim, *The Prayers of Jesus*, Naperville, Allenson, Inc., 1967- Chapter 1, "Abba," pp. 11-65.

Kessler, J.B.A., Jr., *A Study of the Older Protestant Missions and Churches in Peru and Chile*, Goes, Oostervaan & le Cointre N.V., 1967.

Kim, Okgill, quoted in minutes of *Asia Evangelical Theological Consultation*, Singapore, July 5-7, 1970.

Kinsler, F. Ross, "Extend the Seminaries," chapter in *Theological Education by Extension*, CAMEO, East Lansing, 1970, pp. 245-255.

_____, *What is Extension?* mimeographed paper published as *Theological Monograph #3*, Theological Assistance Program of the World Evangelical Fellowship, October, 1970, p. 4.

Lalive d'Epinay, Christian, "The Training of Pastors and Theological Education, the Case of Chile," *International Review of Missions*, Geneva, WCC, Vol. LVI, No. 222, April, 1967, pp. 185-192.

Lange, Phil C. and Desmond P. Wedberg, "The Feasability of Programmed Learning for Developing Countries," *Audio-Visual Instruction*, April, 1970, pp. 65-67.

Latourette, Kenneth Scott, A History of the Expansion of Christianity, Vol. 1, The First Five Centuries, New York, Harper, 1937.

_____, The Unquenchable Light, New York, Harper, 1941.

McCullah, Gerald (ed.), The Ministry in the Methodist Heritage, Nashville Board of Education of the Methodist Church, 1960.

McGavran, Donald A., How Churches Grow, London, World Dominion Press, 1959.

_____, "Ten Prominent Elements in the Church Growth Point of View," *Evangelical Missions Quarterly*, Vol. 3, Fall, 1966, p. 23.

McKay, Arthur, "McCormick Theological Seminary—" *Nexus*, Vol. 12, Spring, 1969, pp. 27-30.

Meadowcroft, John G., *Theological Education by Extension*, mimeographed paper, Gujranwala, West Pakistan, 1970.

Ministry of Education and Culture, Israel, School Comes to Adults, Jerusalem, 1965.

Morris, Raymond, "Report on Potosi Extension Department," *Minutes of the Meeting of the Board of Directors of the George Allan Theological Seminary* (translated from Spanish), October 13, 1970, p. 7.

Muirhead, Ian, Education in the New Testament, New York: Association Press, 1965, Chapter 3, pp. 49-64.

Nicholls, Bruce J., *Theological Education in India*, mimeographed paper prepared for Extension Seminary Workshop, September, 1970, Yoetmal, India.

Niebuhr, Richard and Daniel Williams, eds., The Ministry in Historical Perspective, New York, Harper, 1956.

Norwood, Frederick, "Americanization of the Wesleyan Itinerant," in Gerald McCullah (ed.), The Ministry in the Methodist Heritage, Nashville, Board of Education of the Methodist Church, 1960, p. 55.

Bibliography

Office of Worldwide Evangelism in Depth, *In Depth Evangelism Around the World*, Miami, Latin America Mission, September-October, 1970.

"The Open University," *Expository Times*, April, 1970- 81:70, p. 224.

Packer, J. I., Evangelism and the Sovereignty of God, Chicago: IVCF Press, 1961, p. 48.

Parry, Scott B., "What the West Africans Taught Us About P.I.," *Programmed Instruction*, Vol. 4, April, 1965.

Ransom, C. W., The Christian Minister in India, His Vocation and Training, London, Lutterworth Press, 1946.

Read, William R., Victor M. Monterroso and Harmon A. Johnson, Latin American Church Growth, Grand Rapids, Eerdmans, 1969.

Rivas, Mario, "Nueva Vision de la Iglesia Nacional," article in *Chasqui*, Los Angeles, September, 1970.

Ro, Bong Rin, "Some Thoughts on the Future of Theological Education in Asia," *The Asian Challenge*, Vol. 2, September, 1970.

Roller, Otto, Das Formular Der Paulinischen Briefe, Stuggart: W. Kohlhammer, 1933.

Rowen, Samuel F., "Let's Train the Right People," *Whitened Harvest*, Coral Gables, West Indies Mission, Fall, 1968, Supplement.

Savage, Peter, letter to Dr. Ted Ward, November 4, 1970.

Shearer, Roy, Wildfire: Church Growth in Korea, Grand Rapids, Eerdmans, 1966.

Smith, Ebbie, God's Miracles: Indonesian Church Growth, South Pasadena, William Carey Library, 1970.

Thut, I. N. and Don Adams, Educational Patterns in Contemporary Societies, New York, McGraw-Hill, 1964.

Vicedom, George, Report to the Board of Missions of the Presbyterian Church in Canada, 1958.

Vergara, Ignacio, El protestantismo en Chile, Santiago, Editorial del Pacifico, 1962.

Ward, Ted and Margaret, <u>Programmed Instruction for Theological Education by Extension</u>, East Lansing, CAMEO, 1970.

Ward, Ted, *The Split Rail Fence: An Analogy for the Education of Professionals*, East Lansing, College of Education, Michigan State University, 1969.

Webster, Douglas, "A Time for Honesty about the Ministry," *International Review of Missions*, Geneva, WCC, Vol. LII, October, 1963.

Willems, Emilio, <u>Followers of the New Faith</u>, Vanderbilt University Press, 1967.

Winter, Ralph D., ed., <u>Theological Education by Extension</u>, South Pasadena, William Carey Library, 1969.

____, "A Revolution Goes into Orbit," *World Vision Magazine*, Vol. 14, November, 1970.

____, *El Seminario de Extension en Guatemala*, El Seminario de Extension, informe del cursillo en Cochabamba, Bolivia, del 3 al 7 de agosto, 1968.

____, "New Winds Blowing," <u>Church Growth Bulletin, Volumes I-V</u>, Donald A. McGavran, ed., South Pasadena, William Carey Library, 1969, p. 242.

____, "This Seminary Goes to the Student," *World Vision Magazine*, July-August, 1966, p. 11.

INDEX

"Abba," 36
Academic requirements, 10
Africa
    General situation, 119 f.
    Initial experiments, 120
Andes Evangelical Mission, 78
Anonymous Christians, 17
Armenia, Colombia, 77, 82, 111
Assemblies of God, 113, 128
Athayal, 124
Asia
    General situation, 120 f.
    Initial experiments, 122 f.
    Misunderstandings, 123
    Problems, 124

Barrett, David, 127
Berlin Congress on Evangelism, 128
Biddulph, Burt, 82
Body of Christ, 22, 27
Bolivia, 78 ff.
Bradshaw, 3
Brazil, 83, 116
Buker, 1

Call to ministry, 31
CAMEO, ix, 1, 118
CATA, 112, 114 ff.
C. & M.A., 82, 122
Church
    Base for theological education, 12
    Changing patterns, 2 f.
    Seen in Acts, 15 f.
    Nature of, 15 ff.
CLATT, 112 ff.
COFAE, 124
Colombia, 81 ff.
Confucian system, 121
Congresses on Evangelism, 128
Covell, Ralph, x, 118
Cultural factors, 9 f.
Curriculum
    Current modifications, 99
    Planning at Armenia, 111 f.

Discipleship Training Center, 93
Dodd, C. H., 18

Echeverria, Raul, 74
Economic factors, 11 f., 130
Education
    Progressive, 103, 105 ff.
    Traditional, 103 ff.
    Theological vs. Christian, 29 f.
EFMA-IFMA, 120
Emery, James, 8, 72, 113
Espich and Williams, 115
Ethiopia, 120
Evangelical Union of South America, 77
Evangelism Deep-and-Wide, 128
Extension Education
    Centers George Allan Seminary, 79 ff.
    Combined with residence, 97
    Description of a model center, 85 ff.
    New Experiments, 95 ff.
    Philosophy of, 6 ff.
    Possible shortcomings, 93 ff.
    Relationship to Church Growth, 128 ff.
    Relation to Gifts of Holy Spirit, 26 ff.
    Relation to teacher, 37
    Requirements for a center, 90 f.
    Use by Fuller Seminary, 60

Fruit of Holy Spirit, 26
Fuller Seminary, 60

George Allan Theological Seminary, 12, 79 ff., 96 ff.
Gifts of the Holy Spirit, 25 ff.
Gospel Missionary Union, 83
Guatemala, 1, 71 ff., 95

Hilgeman, George, 79

Honduras Extension Bible Institute, 130
Hoover, Willis, 63
Hopewell, James, 21

India, 123
Indigenous theology, 49
Indonesia, 122 f.
Intertexts, 110 ff.
Israeli government, 2

Jesus
　Authority, 36
　Delegating work, 40
　Evaluating His disciples, 39
　Lord of Church, 17, 22
　Prayer life, 35 f.
　Teaching method, 35 ff.

Kavanagh, Philip, 98
Kim, 9 f.
Kinsler, Ross, 1, 72, 113 f.

Lalive, Christian, 66
<u>Latin American Church Growth</u>, 70
Latourette, Kenneth, 53, 127
Leadership
　Mature, 6 f., 19 f., 130
　Chilean Pentecostals, 65 ff.
Learning
　Types of, 102
　Levels of, 102 f.
Lecture, 104
Library, 86, 91, 94

Mager, Robert, 115
McCormick Theological Seminary, 59
McGavran, Donald, 3, 129
McIntosh, Stewart, 99
Memory, 50, 103, 105
Mennonite Brethren, 83
Ministry, changing, 3 ff.
Monthly meetings, 96
Morris, Raymond, 79, 97

National Liberty Foundation, 118

Nicholls, Bruce, 120, 124
Nigeria, 120

Open University, 2, 60
Ordination "gap," 4, 170 f.
Oriental Missionary Society, 81

Paul
　Principles of teaching, 45 ff.
　Selectivity in training, 48
　Sources of his message, 45 f.
　Terms to describe his teaching, 45
　Viewed self as teacher, 44
Peninsula Bible Church, 25
Pentecostalism in Chile, 64 f., 128
Prayer, 35 f.
Pre-Seminary training, 74

Quechua training, 78 f.

Ray, Chandu, 124
Rehner, Wallace, 112
Reimer, Vernon, 82
Rhodesia, 120
Rivas, 4
Rowen, Sam, 118 f.
Ruanda system, 128

St. Paul School of Theology, 59
Savage, Peter, 78, 89 f., 96, 113 f., 116
Self-instructional materials, 73 f., 105 ff., 110 ff., 119, 123
Seminary, ecclesiastical definition, 81
Singapore consultation, 9 f., 124
Smith, 4
Soka Gakkai, 121
South American Mission, 81
Sturz, Richard, 83, 116

Taiwan
　"Double the Church," 21
　Hakka training, 129

Index

Mountain movement, 41 f., 46 f.
Extension workshops, 122
Yuli Theological Institute, 129
Teaching
  Authority of teacher, 104 f.
  By example, 35 ff.
  By evaluation, 39
  Christ-centered, 48 f.
  Culturally relevant, 47 f., 130 f.
  Emphasizing principles, 49 f.
  Function of in centers, 86, 88
  Going from known to unknown, 38
  In concentrated periods, 97 f.
  In life situations, 37
  Lecture method, 37 f., 104
  Lengthened contact students, 97
  Personalized, 38
  Relation to evangelism, 45
  Relation to obedience, 46 f.
  Shortened contact students, 98
  Teaching laymen, 96
Theological Education
  Current experiments, 58 ff.
  Early American, 56 ff.
  Episcopal schools, 54
  Form vs. function, 52 f.
  In Alexandria, 53
  Levels of training, 85, 111 f.
  Monasteries, 54
  New Testament period, 53
  Reformation period, 54 f.
  17th century England, 55 f.

United Biblical Seminary, 81 ff.
United World Mission, 81
Urban Ministry Program, 59

Vasquez, Javier, 64
Vietnam, 122

Wagner, Peter, x, 118, 121
Ward, Ted, 1, 107 f., 115, 118 f.
Weekly visits, 96, 108
Weld, Wayne, 82, 114 f.
Winter, Ralph, 1, 72, 75, 108, 116, 131
Workshops, extension
  Asia, 119 ff.
  Africa, 119 ff.

Yuli Theological Institute, 129

ABOUT THE WILLIAM CAREY LIBRARY

William Carey is widely considered the "Father of Modern Missions" partly because many people think he was the first Protestant missionary. Even though there was a trickle of others before him, he deserves very special honor for many valiant accomplishments in his heroic career, but most particularly because of three things he did before he ever left England, things no one else in history before him had combined together:

    1) he had an authentic, personal, evangelical passion to serve God and acknowledged this as obligating him to fulfill God's interests in the redemption of all men on the face of the earth.

    2) he actually proposed a structure for the accomplishment of that aim - he did indeed, more than anyone else, set off the movement among Protestants for the creation of "voluntary societies" for foreign missions, and

    3) he added to all of this a strategic literary and research achievement: shaky those statistics may have been, but he put together the very best possible estimate of the number of unreached peoples in every part of the globe, and summarized previous, relatively ineffective attempts to reach them. His burning conclusion was that existing efforts were not proportional to the opportunities and the scope of Christian obligation in Mission.

Today, a little over 150 years later, the situation is not wholly different. In the past five years, for example, experienced missionaries from all corners of the earth (53 countries) have brought to the Fuller School of World Mission and Institute of Church Growth well over 800 years of missionary experience. Twenty-six scholarly books have resulted from the research of faculty and students. The best statistics available have at times been shaky -though far superior to Carey's - but vision has been clear and the mandate is as urgent as ever. The printing press is still the right arm of Christians active in the Christian world mission.

The William Carey Library is a new publishing house dedicated to books related to this mission. There are many publishers, both secular and religious, that occasionally publish books of this kind. We believe there is no other devoted exclusively to the production and distribution of books for career missionaries and their home churches.

William Carey Library
PUBLICATIONS

Africa

PEOPLES OF SOUTHWEST ETHIOPIA, by A. R. Tippett, Ph.D.
   A recent, penetrating evaluation by a professional anthropologist of the cultural complexities faced by Peace Corps workers and missionaries in a rapidly changing intersection of African states.
   1970: 320 pp, $3.95. ISBN 0-87808-103-8

PROFILE FOR VICTORY: NEW PROPOSALS FOR MISSIONS IN ZAMBIA, by Max Ward Randall.
   "In a remarkably objective manner the author has analyzed contemporary political, social educational and religious trends, which demand a re-examination of traditional missionary methods and the creation of daring new strategies...his conclusions constitute a challenge for the future of Christian missions, not only in Zambia, but around the world."
   1970: 224 pp, Cloth, $3.95. ISBN 0-87808-403-7

THE CHURCH OF THE UNITED BRETHREN OF CHRIST IN SIERRA LEONE, by Emmett D. Cox, Executive Secretary, United Brethren in Christ Board of Missions.
   A readable account of the relevant historical, demographic and anthropological data as they relate to the development of the United Brethren in Christ Church in the Mende and Creole communities. Includes a reformation of objectives.
   1970: 184 pp, $2.95. ISBN 0-87808-301-4

APPROACHING THE NUER OF AFRICA THROUGH THE OLD TESTAMENT, by Ernest A. McFall.
   The author examines in detail the similarities between the Nuer and the Hebrews of the Old Testament and suggests a novel Christian approach that does not make initial use of the New Testament.
   1970: 104 pp, 8 1/2 x 11, $1.95.
ISBN 0-87808-310-3

Asia

TAIWAN: MAINLINE VERSUS INDEPENDENT CHURCH GROWTH, A STUDY IN CONTRASTS, by Allen J. Swanson.

A provocative comparison between the older, historical Protestant churches in Taiwan and the new indigenous Chinese churches; suggests staggering implications for missions everywhere that intend to promote the development of truly indigenous expressions of Christianity.
1970: 216 pp, $2.95. ISBN 0-87808-404-5

NEW PATTERNS FOR DISCIPLING HINDUS: THE NEXT STEP IN ANDHRA PRADESH, INDIA, by B.V. Subbamma.

Proposes the development of a Christian movement that is as well adapted culturally to the Hindu tradition as the present movement is to the Harijan tradition. Nothing could be more crucial for the future of 400 million Hindus in India today.
1970: 212 pp, $3.45. ISBN 0-87808-306-5

GOD'S MIRACLES: INDONESIAN CHURCH GROWTH, by Ebbie C. Smith, Th.D.

The fascinating details of the penetration of Christianity into the Indonesian archipelago make for intensely interesting reading, as the anthropological context and the growth of the Christian movement are highlighted.
1970: 224 pp, $3.45. ISBN 0-87808-302-2

NOTES ON CHRISTIAN OUTREACH IN A PHILIPPINE COMMUNITY, by Marvin K. Mayers, Ph.D.

The fresh observations of an anthropologist coming from the outside provide a valuable, however preliminary, check list of social and historical factors in the context of missionary endeavors in a Tagalog province.
1970: 71 pp, 8 1/2 x 11, $1.45. ISBN 0-87808-104-6

Latin America

THE PROTESTANT MOVEMENT IN BOLIVIA, by C. Peter Wagner.

An excitingly-told account of the gradual build-up and present vitality of Protestantism. A cogent analysis of the various subcultures and the organizations working most effectively, including a striking evaluation of Bolivia's momentous Evangelism-in-Depth year and the possibilities of Evangelism-in-Depth for other parts of the world.
1970: 264 pp, $3.95. ISBN 0-87808-402-9

LA SERPIENTE Y LA PALOMA, by Manuel Gaxiola.
 The impressive success story of the Apostolic Church of Mexico, (an indigenous denomination that never had the help of any foreign missionary), told by a professional scholar now the director of research for that church. (Spanish)
 1970: 200 pp, $2.95. ISBN 0-87808-802-4

THE EMERGENCE OF A MEXICAN CHURCH: THE ASSOCIATE REFORMED PRESBYTERIAN CHURCH OF MEXICO, by James Erskine Mitchell.
 Tells the ninety-year story of the Associate Reformed Presbyterian Mission in Mexico, the trials and hardships as well as the bright side of the work. Eminently practical and helpful regarding the changing relationship of mission and church in the next decade.
 1970: 184 pp, $2.95. ISBN 0-87808-303-0

FRIENDS IN CENTRAL AMERICA, by Paul C. Enyart.
 This book describes the results of faithful and effective labors of the California Friends Yearly Meeting, giving an analysis of the growth of one of the most virile, national evangelical churches in Central America, comparing its growth to other evangelical churches in Guatemala, Honduras, and El Salvador.
 1970: 224 pp, $3.45. ISBN 0-87808-405-3

Europe

THE CHALLENGE FOR EVANGELICAL MISSIONS TO EUROPE: A SCANDINAVIAN CASE STUDY, by Hilkka Malaska.
 Graphically presents the state of Christianity in Scandinavia with an evaluation of the pros and cons and possible contributions that existing or additional Evangelical missions can make in Europe today.
 1970: 192 pp, $2.95. ISBN 0-87808-308-1

THE PROTESTANT MOVEMENT IN ITALY: ITS PROGRESS, PROBLEMS, AND PROSPECTS, by Roger Hedlund.
 A carefully wrought summary of preliminary data; perceptively develops issues faced by Evangelical Protestants in all Roman Catholic areas of Europe. Excellent graphs.
 1970: 266 pp, $3.95. ISBN 0-87808-307-3

U.S.A.

THE YOUNG LIFE CAMPAIGN AND THE CHURCH, by Warren Simandle.

If 70 per cent of young people drop out of the church between the ages of 12 and 20, is there room for a nationwide Christian organization working on high school campuses? After a quarter of a century, what is the record of Young Life and how has its work with teens affected the church? *"A careful analysis based on a statistical survey; full of insight and challenging proposals for both Young Life and the church."*

1970: 216 pp, $3.45. ISBN 0-87808-304-9

THE RELIGIOUS DIMENSION IN SPANISH LOS ANGELES: A PROTESTANT CASE STUDY, by Clifton L. Holland.

A through analysis of the origin, development and present extent of this vital, often unnoticed element in Southern California.

1970: 304 pp, $3.95. ISBN 0-87808-309-X

General

THEOLOGICAL EDUCATION BY EXTENSION, edited by Ralph D. Winter, Ph.D.

A husky handbook on a new approach to the education of pastoral leadership for the church. Gives both theory and practice and the exciting historical development in Latin America of the *"Largest non-governmental voluntary educational development project in the world today."* Ted Ward, Prof. of Education, Michigan State University.

1969: 648 pp, Library Buckram $7.95, Kivar $4.95. ISBN 0-87808-101-1

THE CHURCH GROWTH BULLETIN, VOL. I-V, edited by Donald A. McGavran, Ph.D.

The first five years of issues of a now-famous bulletin which probes past foibles and present opportunities facing the 100,000 Protestant and Catholic missionaries in the world today. No periodical edited for this audience has a larger readership.

1969: 408 pp, Library Buckram $6.95, Kivar $4.45. ISBN 0-87808-701-X

CHURCH GROWTH THROUGH EVANGELISM-IN-DEPTH, by Malcolm R. Bradshaw.
"*Examines the history of Evangelism-in-Depth and other total mobilization approaches to evangelism. Also presents concisely the 'Church Growth' approach to mission and proposes a wedding between the two...a great blessing to the church at work in the world.*" WORLD VISION MAGAZINE.
1969: 152 pp, $2.45. ISBN 0-87808-401-0

THE TWENTY FIVE UNBELIEVABLE YEARS, 1945-1969, by Ralph D. Winter, Ph.D.
A terse, exciting analysis of the most significant transition in human history in this millenium and its impact upon the Christian movement. "*Packed with insight and otherwise unobtainable statistical data...a brilliant piece of work.*" C. Peter Wagner.
1970: 120 pp, $1.95. ISBN 0-87808-102-X

EL SEMINARIO DE EXTENSION: UN MANUAL, by James H. Emery, F. Ross Kinsler, Louise J. Walker, Ralph D. Winter.
Gives the reasons for the extension approach to the training of ministers, as well as the concrete, practical details of establishing and operating such a program. A Spanish translation of the third section of *THEOLOGICAL EDUCATION BY EXTENSION*.
1969: 256 pp, $3.45. ISBN 0-87808-801-6